The Mirror of Mindfulness

RANGJUNG YESHE BOOKS • *www.rangjung.com*

PADMASAMBHAVA: *Treasures from Juniper Ridge* •
Advice from the Lotus-Born • *Dakini Teachings* •
Following in Your Footsteps: The Lotus-Born Guru in Nepal •
Following in Your Footsteps: The Lotus-Born Guru in India

PADMASAMBHAVA AND JAMGÖN KONGTRÜL:
The Light of Wisdom, Vol. 1, Vol. 2, Vol. 3, Secret, Vol. 4 & Vol. 5

PADMASAMBHAVA, CHOKGYUR LINGPA, JAMYANG KHYENTSE WANGPO,
TULKU URGYEN RINPOCHE, ORGYEN TOBGYAL RINPOCHE, & OTHERS
Dispeller of Obstacles • *The Tara Compendium* • *Powerful Transformation* •
Dakini Activity

YESHE TSOGYAL: *The Lotus-Born*

DAKPO TASHI NAMGYAL: *Clarifying the Natural State*

TSELE NATSOK RANGDRÖL: *Mirror of Mindfulness* • *Heart Lamp*

CHOKGYUR LINGPA: *Ocean of Amrita* • *The Great Gate* • *Skillful Grace* •
Great Accomplishment • *Guru Heart Practices*

TRAKTUNG DUDJOM LINGPA: *A Clear Mirror*

JAMGÖN MIPHAM RINPOCHE:
Gateway to Knowledge, Vol. 1, Vol. 2, Vol. 3, & Vol. 4

TULKU URGYEN RINPOCHE: *Blazing Splendor* • *Rainbow Painting* •
As It Is, Vol. 1 & Vol. 2 • *Vajra Speech* • *Repeating the Words of the Buddha* •
Dzogchen Deity Practice • *Vajra Heart Revisited*

ADEU RINPOCHE: *Freedom in Bondage*

KHENCHEN THRANGU RINPOCHE: *Crystal Clear*

CHÖKYI NYIMA RINPOCHE: *Bardo Guidebook* •
Collected Works of Chökyi Nyima Rinpoche, Vol. 1 & Vol. 2

TULKU THONDUP: *Enlightened Living*

ORGYEN TOBGYAL RINPOCHE: *Life & Teachings of Chokgyur Lingpa* •
Straight Talk • *Sublime Lady of Immortality*

DZIGAR KONGTRÜL RINPOCHE: *Uncommon Happiness*

TSOKNYI RINPOCHE: *Fearless Simplicity* • *Carefree Dignity*

MARCIA BINDER SCHMIDT: *Dzogchen Primer* • *Dzogchen Essentials* •
Quintessential Dzogchen • *Confessions of a Gypsy Yogini* •
Precious Songs of Awakening Compilation

ERIK PEMA KUNSANG: *Wellsprings of the Great Perfection* •
A Tibetan Buddhist Companion • *The Rangjung Yeshe Tibetan-English
Dictionary of Buddhist Culture & Perfect Clarity*

The Mirror of Mindfulness

THE CYCLE OF THE FOUR BARDOS

Tsele Natsok Rangdröl

TRANSLATED BY
Erik Pema Kunsang

FOREWORDS BY
H. H. Dilgo Khyentse Rinpoche
and
Ven. Tulku Chökyi Nyima Rinpoche

INTRODUCTORY DISCOURSE BY
Ven. Tulku Urgen Rinpoche

RANGJUNG YESHE PUBLICATIONS
Boudhanath, Hong Kong & århus

Rangjung Yeshe Publications
125 Robinson Rd, flat 6a
Hong Kong

www.rangjung.com
rangjung@earthlink.net

Address letters to:

Rangjung Yeshe Publications
Ka-Nying Shedrub Ling Monastery
P.O. Box 1200, Kathmandu, Nepal

FIRST EDITION 1987

Printed in the United States of America
Distributed to the Book Trade by
North Atlantic Books & Random House

Publication Data:

Tsele Natsok Rangdrol (Rtse-Le Rgod-Tshang-Pa, Sna Tshogs Rang Grol,
b. 1608). *The Mirror Of Mindfulness: The Cycle Of The Four Bardos*
The Final Words of Tsele Natsok Rangdrol
Translated from the Tibetan by Erik Pema Kunsang (Erik Hein Schmidt)
Edited by Marcia Binder Schmidt
Foreword by His Holliness Dilgo Khyentse
and Ven. Chokyi Nyima Rinpoche (b. 1951)
Introductory discourse by Tulku Urgyen Rinpoche (1920–1996)
Title: *The Mirror Of Mindfulness*

ISBN 978–962–7341–65–9 (PBK.)

1. Mahayana and Vajrayana — tradition of pith instructions.
2. Buddhism — Tibet. I. Title.
bar do spyi'i donthams cad gsal bar byed pa dran pa'i me long bzhugs so.

Cover Art Design courtesy of Maryann Lipaj

Tsele Natsok Rangdrol

CONTENTS

FOREWORD

BY His Holiness Dilgo Khyentse

THE MOST LEARNED TSELE PEMA LEGDRUB was the body-emanation of the great translator Vairochana, and he attained the pinnacle of learning and accomplishment of the masters of the Land of Snow. Also known as Kongpo Gotsang Natsok Rangdröl, he was unmatched in his three qualities of scholarship, virtue, and noble-mindedness.

Among the five volumes of his collected works, I considered that this explanation of the bardos would benefit everyone interested in the dharma. The words are clear and easy to understand, and lengthy scholarly expositions are not emphasized. This text, easy to comprehend and containing all the key points and very direct instructions, results from following the oral advice of a qualified master.

In order to help the foreigners who are presently interested in the dharma to gain true confidence, I, old Dilgo Khyentse, encouraged my disciple Erik Pema Kunsang to translate this book into English. Therefore, may everyone trust in this.

Written on the twenty-fifth day of the first month of the year of the Earth Dragon.

FOREWORD

BY Tulku Chökyi Nyima

I HAVE CHOSEN *The Mirror of Mindfulness* by Tsele Natsok Rangdrol as the text for the 1987 seminar, for several
reasons. Primarily the subject matter, death and rebirth, is
a very important and pertinent topic for both Buddhists
and non-Buddhists. Tibetan Buddhism contains many
books which encompass teachings on that topic, and this
text is especially suitable, as it is easy to understand. The
author's style is very clear, precise, and direct.

Both H. H. Dilgo Khyentse Rinpoche and Tulku Urgyen Rinpoche have recommended *The Mirror of Mindfulness* for my students to study, so I decided to make it
available on a wider scale. Therefore, please read it carefully and take the meaning to heart.

I pray that an understanding of these teachings may be
of benefit to all beings.

KA-NYING SHEDRUP LING MONASTERY
BOUDHANATH, NEPAL
SEPTEMBER 1987

TRANSLATOR'S PREFACE

THIS TEXT is a translation of *The Mirror of Mindfulness*,[1] a commentary on the bardo states that is well known to advanced practitioners in Tibet. Together with Tsele Natsok Rangdröl's works on the Mahamudra and Dzogchen systems, it forms a trilogy that encompasses the most subtle oral instructions of vajrayana practice. It is the aspiration of Tulku Chökyi Nyima Rinpoche that these important texts be made available to English-speaking practitioners.

The author, Tsele Natsok Rangdröl, was born near the border of the Tibetan provinces Kongpo and Dakpo in the year 1608. He was recognized as a reincarnation of Gotsangpa, a great master of the Drukpa Kagyü lineage and an emanation of Milarepa. In his youth he studied with the Third Pawo Rinpoche and the famous tertön Jatsön Nyingpo as well as other great teachers of the Kagyü and Nyingma lineages.

The following autobiographical information about Tsele Natsok Rangdröl was extracted by His Holiness Dilgo Khyentse from the inner life story of Jamgön Kongtrül the First. According to that text, Tsele Rinpoche is counted among the succession of Jamgön Kongtrül's past incarnations:

> The most learned master Tsele Padma Legdrub Natsok Rangdröl was prophesied as the body-emanation of the great translator Vairochana. Renowned as the reincar-

---

1. The full Tibetan title is *Bar do spyi'i don thams cad rnam pa gsal bar byed pa dran pa'i me long* (*The Mirror of Mindfulness: A Clarification of the General Points of the Bardos*).

nation of the incomparable Tendzin Dorje, he was invited to the Thangdruk Monastery established by his previous incarnation. Attending numerous learned and accomplished masters, including Gangra Lochen, he fully comprehended the philosophical scriptures and oral instructions of sutra and tantra, according to the new and old schools. As he was extremely disciplined, even the liquor in his feast offerings was prepared from water with molasses. His tongue never touched a drop of alcohol.

In the latter part of his life he stayed in Palri Götsang, the cave of Deshek Tse in the south, and other places where he perfected the realization of Mahamudra and Dzogchen. Among his disciples are included Gampopa Sangpo Dorje, Bomting Chöje Miphampa, Tau Pema Lodrö, and others.

The Bardo teachings from both of these lineages are joined in *The Mirror of Mindfulness,* which connects the key points of the view, meditation, and practice to the four bardos in a way that can be applied to a student's individual level of meditation experience.

This practical guidebook on how to face all events during life and death takes as its main theme the four bardos that together cover the whole cycle of living, dying, the after-death state, and taking rebirth. The book explains these four bardos in the following chapters:

1. The natural bardo of this life.
2. The painful bardo of dying.
3. The luminous bardo of dharmata.
4. The karmic bardo of becoming.

What does the Tibetan word *bardo* mean? It literally means "intermediate state," the gap or period between two events, a transition period in the series of changes a sentient being undergoes in an endless chain of births and deaths called samsara.

In order to read this book with an open mind, one must reevaluate the worldview of materialistic nihilism that most Westerners have been brought up with and for the most part simply take for granted. If one decides that a human being is merely one of nature's accidents, a biological organism which is born, tries to survive and reproduce, and then dies, leaving nothing but a corpse of material particles, then there is not much opportunity for spirituality. This nihilistic viewpoint is based on ordinary people's perceptions.

An enlightened being like Buddha Shakyamuni, on the other hand, teaches according to an extraordinary insight into life and reality. This enlightened insight can be tested through one's own experience. The Buddha taught that the physical body is only a temporary abode, an excellent dwelling in fact, but nevertheless not so important as the inhabitant, the consciousness, which is a continual stream of cognition.

At present our consciousness is temporarily in a human body. However, this condition of being embodied lasts for an uncertain length of time. This is the first intermediate state, the natural bardo of this life.

After being born, growing up, leading a life, and maybe growing old, the body dies but not the mind. For a certain period the consciousness undergoes a separation from the embodied state and enters a state totally without solid grounding. That is the second intermediate state, the painful bardo of dying.

The basis for consciousness is not compounded by material particles and therefore not subject to their change or transformation. Nonetheless, unlike physical space, it has a cognitive capacity which gives rise to manifestation. During the third intermediate state, the luminous bardo of dharmata, one is disembodied, that is, without any physical support whatsoever. The mind is utterly bare and naked; there is only dharmata, "what naturally is." In this state, it is said, perception and experience are seven times more vivid than usual. Consequently, the opportunity for either confusion or clarity is intensified seven times. The manifestations of one's basic nature, dharmata, can be experienced either as a nightmare of haunting demons or as a pure realm of divine beings.

When habitual tendencies of grasping at duality—which stem from lack of insight into the basic nature of mind and are embedded in one's base of consciousness—regain power after their short lapse, one seeks reembodiment corresponding to one's karmic habits, which are now ready to ripen. That is the fourth intermediate state, the karmic bardo of becoming.

After a while one enters a new body, not necessarily human, and is again in the first bardo.

This cycle of the four bardos goes on endlessly, unless one is born as a human being and connects with the right teacher and teachings. The goals and aims that are paramount in the first bardo, such as wealth, power, social position, and fame, seem futile and pointless when one recognizes that these mundane attainments are all left behind in passing through the other bardos.

But *The Mirror of Mindfulness* is not merely an esoteric lesson in the pointlessness and futility of worldly concerns. Tsele Natsok Rangdröl gives the key points of the Practice Lineage on dealing with the situation in each of the four bardos—that is, how to face the situation directly and take advantage of the opportunities that each bardo presents, in accordance with the oral teachings of the lineage masters.

The Buddha taught the following conditions for liberation from the cycle of samsaric rebirths and the attainment of enlightenment for the welfare of others: being a human being, meeting a qualified master, receiving the oral instructions, and applying them to one's experience through practice. This book summarizes such oral instructions and offers practical advice that is meant to be taken personally. The general reader may find many unusual terms in this text because it was written by a practitioner of the most subtle and profound Buddhist teachings for other practitioners of such teachings. Words and expressions are therefore used which require explanation by a qualified master. The glossary at the end of the book may also be of some help, as it includes the Tibetan version of the terms.

There are a few books on the four bardos available in English which I would like to recommend:

> *The Rain of Wisdom,* by the Nālandā Translation Committee under the direction of Chögyam Trungpa (Shambhala Publications, 1980; 1988), covers most of the teachings relating to the first bardo, the natural bardo of this life.

> *The Tibetan Book of the Dead: The Great Liberation through Hearing in the Bardo,* translated with commentary by Francesca Fremantle and Chögyam Trungpa (Shambhala Publications, 1987), covers the last three bardos.

> *Union of Mahamudra and Dzogchen* by Chökyi Nyima Rinpoche, Seminar 1985 (Rangjung Yeshe Publications, 1986), covers all four bardos.

ACKNOWLEDGMENTS

The occasion for this translation was the seventh annual fall seminar on Buddhist theory and practice held at Rangjung Yeshe Institute in Boudhanath, October 1987. According to the advice of H. H. Dilgo Khyentse, Tulku

Translator's Preface

Chökyi Nyima Rinpoche expressed his wish to use *The Mirror of Mindfulness* as the basis for his series of talks, and so I undertook the task of translating this work. During the process of refining it, we relied on the precious oral instructions of Tulku Urgyen and Chökyi Nyima Rinpoche for clarifying obscure points in the text.

I would like to thank these teachers and all the friends who gave their time and energy, especially my wife, Marcia Schmidt, for correcting against the Tibetan text, Judy and Wayne Amtzis for editing, as well as Ani Lodro, George MacDonald, Andreas Kretschmar, Bo Colomby, and Donna Holley for their useful suggestions.

ERIK PEMA KUNSANG
KA-NYING SHEDRUP LING MONASTERY
BOUDHANATH, SEPTEMBER 1987

INTRODUCTORY DISCOURSE

QUITE A FEW WESTERNERS wonder why the intermediate state after death is described by Tibetan teachers as being terrifying, horrible to go through, a frightening experience filled with intense lights, colors, and sounds, when, at the same time, research done by Western hypnotists suggests that the after-death experience is very pleasant, without any discomfort or hardship. In reply I ask, "Are people under hypnosis actually dead?" No, they are not; they are still breathing, whereas a dead person does not breathe. Those hypnotized have only an imitation, only a flickering mental imprint of death, not the actual, immediate experience.

The author of this text, Tsele Natsok Rangdröl, was an extremely learned and accomplished master of Tibet, rivaling the fame of Longchen Rabjam and Mipham Rinpoche. He was also known as Götsangpa ("Vulture Nest Dweller") because he spent long periods of time in the retreat places, caves, and mountain hermitages of the great Drukpa Kagyü master Götsang Gönpo Dorje. There he attained accomplishment. A great and eminent master, he fully comprehended all the teachings of the schools of Tibetan Buddhism, especially Kagyü and Nyingma. He is said to have perceived the teachings of the Eight Practice Lineages, as well as all of samsara and nirvana, as clearly as something placed in the palm of one's hand. Among his other writings, he also produced expositions of the Mahamudra and Dzogchen systems.

A great number of explanations and commentaries on the bardo states exist. The text here is the most lucid and concise among them. It can be elaborated upon by learned teachers, yet uneducated people also find it easy to understand. All his other works, whether on Mahumudra or Dzogchen, are also unique in this way. Tsele's writings are quite amazing.

Of the different styles of dharma teachings—words of the Buddha and the shastras of the panditas—this text presenting the bardo states is a shastra, a treatise. A shastra elucidates the Buddha's words. In addition, Tsele writes this treatise as an instruction manual rather than as a philosophical treatise. Thus it is more readily understood.

Why should one learn about the bardo state? Usually, we talk about three aspects: the present life, the bardo, and the next life. In the next life, following the intermediate state, we either wander further through samsaric existence, going to one of the higher or lower realms, or attain liberation and enlightenment. Right now we find ourselves in the present life, and the intermediate state, the bardo state, is between the two.

Sometimes six kinds of bardo states are discussed, but they can be condensed into four basic states. The first, the natural bardo of this life, continues from birth until the time of death. The second, the bardo of dying, is the period that begins when we meet with a fatal illness or another cause of death and concludes when we finally expire. The third, the bardo of dharmata, occurs when we have fully passed away. Finally, the bardo of becoming is undergone if we have not recognized our nature in the bardo of dharmata.

In addition to these four bardos, two other bardos occur during this life: the bardo of meditation and the bardo of dreaming. The bardo of meditation is the experience of the meditation state. The bardo of dreaming is the dream state during sleep.

Literally, the Tibetan term for "bardo of this life" means "born and remaining." We have been born from our mother and have not yet passed away. It is the period between birth and death. Here the important point in the daytime is the bardo of meditation, which depends on receiving the oral instructions from a master and training oneself in them. Then, during nighttime, one trains in the bardo of dreaming. If in this way one remains in the bardo of meditation throughout day and night, need one worry about any of the other bardo states? Being adept in the bardos of meditation and dreaming is sufficient. Nothing more remains to be done. But without reaching some degree of stability in meditation and the ability to recognize dreams, I am sorry to say, one cannot avoid enduring the bardo of dying.

A good Dzogchen practitioner, on the other hand, is liberated into the expanse of primordial purity during the bardo of dying. He departs through the Secret Pathway of Vajrasattva before expiring. If one is not stable at that point either, one will arrive at the bardo of dharmata. Here the natural sounds, colors, and lights manifest. *Dharmata* means nature, the unconditioned. The sounds, colors, and lights are unconditioned; they manifest yet they are devoid of self-nature. If one also lacks stability in the bardo of dharmata, sadly enough, one will wander further down into the samsaric circle of seeking another rebirth within the six realms.

As I mentioned earlier, being liberated into the expanse of primordial purity at the moment of death is best. At this point one will go through the experiences of appearance, increase, and attainment. The first of these three experiences, the whiteness of appearance, occurs with the descent of the white element obtained from one's father. The second experience, the redness of increase, occurs with the ascent of the red element obtained from one's mother. The third experience occurs when these two elements meet at one's heart center. The third experience is the actual moment of death.

What follows the moment of this third experience is the fourth experience, the so-called ground luminosity of full attainment. A scripture states: "Then dawns the unconditioned wakefulness of bliss and emptiness." The wakefulness is empty as well as blissful, and if one can recognize it, it is exactly the mahamudra of bliss and emptiness, the mahasandhi of awareness and emptiness, or the madhyamika of appearance and emptiness.

In most cases, however, following the three experiences of the whiteness of appearance, the redness of increase, and the blackness of attainment, one's consciousness, also called prana-mind, faints in the black experience of the white and red elements meeting together in the heart center.

This moment of unconsciousness is for all ordinary people simply an oblivious state, lasting for the most part about three and a half days. On the morning of the fourth day, manifestations suddenly unfold as if the sky and earth were rent asunder. One has been unconscious, totally oblivious, not noticing anything up to this point, so one will wonder, "What happened?"

Conventionally, this is of three days' duration, but there is actually no fixed measure. For those familiar with meditation, it lasts for as long as their meditation state, the duration of nondistraction from mind-essence. For people without training in recognizing mind-essence, these "days" just flash past. For those with virtue and evil in equal measure, the duration is approximately three days. What actually happens at this point is that the fourth experience, the ground luminosity of full attainment, is not recognized and one falls unconscious. That happens for most beings. Quite a few people suffer at this moment because of their intense panic and fear of death. A cry of anguish follows, and then they lose consciousness.

After the passing of three and a half days, one awakens from this oblivious state wondering, "What has happened to me?" The consciousness then leaves the body through one of the eight or nine apertures. It seems quite strange that the mind, which is without any concrete substance, must leave through an opening of the body.

If the mind departs through the top of the head, it is said that one goes to the higher realms or continues on the path of liberation. In fact, there are several openings on the top of the head. One leads to the Formless Realm, another to the Realm of Form, and yet another to the pure lands.

After the consciousness has separated from the body, it will, in the bardo of becoming, go to one of the six realms in keeping with one's individual karma.

According to the system of Karling Shitro, everything happens within a time span of forty-nine days: the peaceful deities manifest in the first week, the wrathful ones in the second week, and so forth. But actually, nothing is definite about those days. For some people everything just flickers by; for others it might happen slowly. Time and occurrence remain unfixed.

On the other hand, if one is a trained practitioner, one will recognize, "This is the experience of appearance!" when the whiteness appears, bright and vivid. And when the experience of redness occurs, one will know, "This is the redness!" Finally, when everything goes black, one will acknowledge, "This is the attainment, the blackness!"

After these three experiences, one will also recognize when the ground luminosity of full attainment manifests like a lamp within a vase. At first, there is an instant of fainting while the eighty inherent thought states cease. Nothing accompanies the cessation of all thought states but nonconceptual wakefulness, awareness wisdom as bright as a lamp in a vase. It is cognizant, nonconceptual, and remains one-pointedly—the union of luminosity and emptiness. That is the ground luminosity, which is like a mother. This means that dharmata, self-existing wakeful-ness, the sugatagarbha, is like a mother. The recognition of it, which one's master has pointed out, is like a child. At this moment the mother and child reunite. The tradi-tional analogy is that it is "like a child jumping into its mother's lap." People who are experienced in such practice understand this, and everything stands and falls with that understanding.

At present, the vital point in our practice is to recognize the nature of awareness. We hear statements such as "Rec-ognize your awareness!" or "He has recognized rigpa, the awareness." Having recognized awareness during one's lifetime, the key point here is to remain in it—to refrain from losing its continuity. At the instant of the cessation of the eighty inherent thought states, self-existing wake-fulness is vividly present—like pure and refined gold, the purity by itself. One can recognize it fully and completely. That is how it has been taught.

This moment has been spoken of thus: "One instant makes the difference. In one instant complete enlighten-ment." In the moment of recognition one can attain full enlightment. That is the meaning of the statement "The best practitioner attains buddhahood in the dharmakaya at the moment of death.'

If one cannot recognize in that way, however, the next

bardo, the bardo of dharmata, will manifest. After the elements and the consciousness have dissolved into space, the stages of space dissolve into luminosity, luminosity dissolves into wisdom, and wisdom dissolves into unity. *Unity* here means the peaceful and wrathful deities. Following that, unity dissolves into spontaneous presence.

Spontaneous presence refers to that which is originally or inherently present within the ground of primordial purity. Some people wonder, "Where do all these deities and lights come from?" They are manifestations of the wakefulness of spontaneous presence. In the practice of Thögal, as well as in the bardo of dharmata, many deities appear. Those deities *are* dharmata. They are not conditioned entities but are of an unconditioned nature. Having neither flesh nor blood, they consist of rainbow lights. The key point in the bardo of dharmata is simply to rest in awareness, no matter what happens, and to be able to embrace everything with the mindfulness of awareness-wisdom, without losing the continuity of that awareness. Without such ability, this bardo lasts no longer than a few flickering moments.

The son of Khakhyab Dorje, the Fifteenth Karmapa, was known as Dungse Jampa Rinpoche. He wasn't much of a practitioner at first, but as he was born in the bloodline of the Karmapa, he was possibly a gifted being. He was also the brother of Jamgön Rinpoche, the second Kongtrül. While working in Lhasa, he fell very ill and almost passed away. With medical treatment, he came back to life in the presence of his brother Jamgön Rinpoche. At that time he received the key points of oral instructions from his brother and was able to clear away all doubts and misconceptions. During the remaining month of his life he trained so diligently and enhanced his initial recognition of the nature of awareness to such an extent that when he finally did pass away, he died in the recognition of mind-essence. Three days before dying, he told Jamgön Rinpoche, "When I die now, I will have no trouble whatsoever. None of these experiences will be able to harm me." Jamgön Rinpoche later told me, "He was a politican his whole life, practicing little, but his intense diligence during the last month brought him extremely good results."

Bardo teachings may sound very fascinating and colorful, but the vital point is one's individual practice right now. Why have medicine when sick, if one doesn't use it? Without training, our studies become mere intellectual understanding. If study were sufficient, we could simply lean back and read a book about Dzogchen. In fact, there is no way around actual training.

The reading of *The Liberation through Hearing in the Bardo* aloud for a dead person, according to the system of Karling Shitro, is to remind a practitioner who already possesses prior training. It is definitely necessary. The most important point is that the reader be someone close to the dead person, one with shared samayas. If the deceased becomes irritated with the reader, there will be no benefit. The two people should at best share the same teacher and be compatible. In that case there will be tremendous benefits.

On the other hand, without prior training in recognition of mind-essence, one will be unable to attain stability in the bardo state. A person who never recognized his mind-essence will, in the first place, fail to cut through the fear and misery of dying, and later, when the intense and overwhelming experiences of the sounds, colors, and lights occur, he will be paralyzed with fear. The sounds will roar like one hundred thousand thunderclaps and the lights will shine more brilliantly than one hundred thousand suns. It is not just a dim glimmering light. Those are the sounds, colors, and lights of the bardo of dharmata.

Accompanying this overwhelming display, some simple, cozy, and comforting sounds, colors, and lights also appear to lure one down into the realms of samsara. One will feel drawn to them. One must therefore attain at least some degree of stability through practice right now.

People with no training at all can also find some benefit from this teaching. In connection with this, there is a story about an old lady from Golok in East Tibet. During a ceremony which she had invited a lama to perform at her house, she saw a painted scroll of the peaceful and wrathful deities and exclaimed, "What kind of terrible deity is that? It has a body of a human with the head of snake!" The lama answered, "Not at all! It is the Snake-Headed Goddess, the last of the hundred sacred deities to appear in the bardo. It is your own innate deity." Later on, the old lady died and went through the terrors of the bardo. Finally the Snake-Headed Goddess raised her head, which was the size of Mount Sumeru, and sent forth a tongue swirling through space. At that moment, the old lady recognized her and thought, "This must be the Snake-Headed Goddess which the lama mentioned! I take refuge in her!" The story ends with her being guided to the path of liberation. So there is clearly some benefit for ordinary people from hearing these teachings.

In East Tibet, it was a tradition to read *The Liberation through Hearing in the Bardo* aloud for people during the forty-nine days after death. Many families invited a monk to stay for seven weeks in order to make offerings and read the text aloud slowly once a day. This will definitely benefit the deceased.

It is also important to have confidence in these teachings and to develop the determination to be clear-headed in the bardo, so that one will recognize what takes place. One must have confidence, otherwise all will be lost.

At best, one should receive the pointing-out instruction to recognize the nature of mind from a qualified master. Success in the bardo comes from applying one's present practice of mind-essence at the time of death. Only training dispels the confusion that arises during the bardo state. That is why one must practice the stages of development and completion right now. Recognize this, and then one will experience at death what one is already familiar with through practice.

The profound and skillful means of the vajrayana teachings do not involve imagining the presence of something nonexistent or pretending that something is what it is not. Rather, the deities are an expression of one's spontaneously present wakefulness; they are automatically there, inherent in one's nature. The teachings say, "Spontaneously present wakefulness manifests within the primordially pure essence." One's primordially pure essence is like a mirror, and the manifestations of the spontaneously present wakefulness are like the reflections appearing within it. That is the essential reason for practicing the development stage right now.

Some people say, "What is the need for the development stage? It is all a fabrication anyway!" Later on, when the spontaneous presence manifests, it will be evident what is false and what is real.

The whole reason for receiving bardo teachings has been traditionally described as that of "connecting a broken water pipe." By training right now, one will be able to continue the "flow" of practice through the bardo state to the following life. In the Dzogchen system bardo training is indispensable. If one has already reached perfection in the practice of Thögal, then there is no need for bardo teachings. In this age, however, life is short, diseases are many, and diligence is feeble. Although one may have entered the path of the Great Perfection, without attaining stability in one's practice and not being able to know whether the time of death will arrive suddenly, one definitely needs the instruction on how to "connect the broken water pipe." One will then be able to attain enlightenment in the bardo state, to proceed to a pure buddha field, or at least to gain a rebirth in one of the higher realms. So these are necessary teachings, especially if one meets an untimely death.

When practicing these teachings one must have confidence and trust and be free from doubt. This teaching is like a guide leading the blind in the right direction. To take the hand of such a guide, one needs trust. Without trust, one might lose one's way. With trust, one will reach the destination. This master's words contain no deception. Tsele Natsok Rangdröl wrote this teaching based on the tantras and oral instructions. He did not merely invent it himself.

Finally, but not of the least importance, the complete teachings on how to practice during the different bardo states should be received from a master endowed with the tradition of oral instructions.

TULKU URGYEN RINPOCHE
NAGI GOMPA, NEPAL
SEPTEMBER 1987

The Mirror of
Mindfulness

Prologue

NAMO GURUBHYA. Salutation to my master.

Utterly pure since the beginning and endowed with the
twofold purity,
Dharmakaya is devoid of all the fabrications of existence
and peace.
Its natural radiance, manifesting without obstruction,
unhindered as the play of the peaceful and wrathful
ones,
Sambhogakaya is endowed with the five wisdoms.
Through countless emanations, taming beings in
manifold ways appropriate for those to be tamed,
Nirmanakaya is endowed with the treasury that fulfills all
wishes.
The master who is the inseparability of these, the lord
encompassing all buddha mandalas,
I worship as indivisible from my own mind.

In the essence of the primordial purity of samsara and
nirvana, appearance and existence,
There are no such words as birth or death, joy or sorrow.
How pitiful, then, that those with unrealized minds
undergo numerous miseries,
Trapped in the hollowness of endless and confused
experiences.

In order to liberate them through manifold skillful means,
The forefathers of the Practice Lineage have indeed
elucidated
Countless supreme instructions on the bardos
As an essential extract of the profound and extensive
teachings.

How could there be something to say and what would be
the need
For an ignoramus like myself to utter anything which
could exceed them?

However, since you, a wise person, have asked me,
I shall simply repeat what our forefathers have taught.

In general, all sentient beings dwell exclusively within bardo states, from the initial ground of confusion until realizing the final enlightenment. All the phenomena of ground and path can therefore be simply labeled *bardo*. Still, ordinary people regard the bardo as being neither more nor less than the terrible state of intermediate existence. In *The Liberation through Hearing in the Bardo (Bardo thos grol gyi gdams pa)* according to the Nyingma School of Secret Mantra, and in other texts, six kinds of bardos are defined. Within that classification, the one called the meditation bardo of samadhi did not fit into the thinking of some scholars of later times, who seem to have refuted its inclusion in various ways. But, if all phenomena of samsara and nirvana are of the nature of the bardos, why cannot the meditation state then be called bardo?

Crossing the Dangerous Pathway of the Bardo, given to the dakini Tashi Tseringma by Lord Milarepa, also discusses the general way of guidance in terms of the six bardos. His manner of defining the meditation bardo of samadhi, in particular, does not differ from that in *The Liberation through Hearing.* Thus, the Sarma and the Nyingma schools agree in their viewpoints.

Generally, all the root texts contain various definitions and ways of guidance for the bardos. For instance, the three bardos known as the natural bardo of this life, the painful bardo of dying, and the bardo of dharmata/becoming have been taught, as have the four bardos of the four kayas of union, self-aware wisdom, timely nature, and unmistaken interdependence. There are, as well, many other systems, such as the six bardos of this life, dream, meditation, dying, dharmata, and becoming.

In this context, I will explain the bardo teachings in

terms that I myself have been familiar with. By combining the key points of what is common to both the Sarma and Nyingma schools, I will condense them under these four points in order to make understanding easy:

1. The natural bardo of this life
2. The painful bardo of dying
3. The luminous bardo of dharmata
4. The karmic bardo of becoming

Each will be explained by means of

A. Identifying its essence
B. Explaining in detail its manner of manifestation
C. Pointing out how to apply the instructions

I

The Natural Bardo
of This Life

IDENTIFICATION

WHAT IS MEANT BY "the bardo of this life"? This refers to the period beginning with emergence from one's mother's womb and ending when one is overcome by a cause of death.

WAY OF MANIFESTING

How does the bardo of this life reveal itself and how is it experienced? It appears in individual ways owing to the differences between realized and unrealized beings. That is to say, to the most fortunate, the world and its inhabitants are spontaneously perfect like a mandala. This is because the fortunate ones recognize sights and sounds as being deities and mantras. Since their thoughts manifest as the play of dharmata, everything is the nature of the three kayas. It is so primordially, it appears so right now, and finally it is liberated into that state. This state is called "all-encompassing purity of appearance and existence" and also "the wisdom wheel of whatever is experienced." Pal Khachö[1] and others have called it by such names as "the bardo of the four kayas of union," "the bardo of self-cognizant wakefulness," and so forth. The meditation bardo of samadhi, mentioned above, is also included

---

1. One of the Shamar tulkus, Shamar Khachö Wang Po.

herein and therefore does not need to be explained separately.

Those who have not realized that this is so, the ordinary and ignorant people, follow their tendencies, bad habits, deluded experiences, and solid fixations from birth, continuously, until they catch a fatal disease. They regard the unreal to be real and expect the impermanent to be permanent. They confuse the painful with the pleasant and cling to that. They completely waste their lives away, with nothing but the futile and deludedly attached activities of the eight worldly concerns[2] or with subduing enemies and protecting friends, attachments to self and aversion to others, feeling incomplete and unsatisfied, hoarding and guarding, rearing a family and looking after farm animals. Since this is in fact what most people experience, the nature of the bardo of this life does not transcend this description. At night their corpselike sleep of stupidity, not embraced by any of the key points of the oral instructions, resembles that of a mindless animal. Moreover, from within the sleep the manifold dream experiences of double-delusion appear and sail by, so that the dream bardo of habitual tendencies also falls within the bardo of this life. The *Sutra of the Noble Source of the Precious Ones* states:

> By the power of attachment to wrong thinking,
> All beings are completely tossed about in this [samsara].
> The person who understands the quality of quiescence
> Sees the self-existing tathagata.
> He will fully perceive the supreme qualities of peace.

Thus the difference between realizing and not realizing is extremely great.

---

2. Attachment to gain, pleasure, fame, and praise; aversion to loss, pain, bad reputation, and blame.

The Natural Bardo of This Life

INSTRUCTIONS ON BRINGING THE BARDO OF THIS LIFE INTO THE PATH

The oral instructions of the Nyingma School teach that one should exert oneself in the teachings on cutting doubts and misconceptions through learning and contemplation, like a swallow entering its nest.[3] How does one do that? First one must search for a qualified master and serve him sincerely in many pleasing ways, being free from deceit in body, speech, and mind. One should properly receive the three sets of precepts that are the foundation of the Buddhist teachings and the life-pillar of the path, and should then observe them without being tainted by even the tiniest stain of violations, breach, fault, or downfall.

Studying and reflecting upon all the stages of the vehicles of sutra and tantra without prejudice, one should cast away any partiality and clinging to a certain school of thought. If one goes astray, becoming attached to great learning, one will merely pursue words of sophistry without understanding the actual meaning. One should therefore take to heart and apply to oneself whatever one has learned. The oral instructions of one's master alone embody the root of all learning and reflection, so one should understand and have no doubt about these oral instructions in their entirety.

One who does not abandon worldly pursuits squanders this life. Therefore, completely sever attachments and ties and remain in secluded mountain dwellings. Yet unlike the birds, deer, and other animals in such secluded places, exert body, speech, and mind in what is virtuous. Give yourself no cause for regret and gain the confidence of not falling prey to ordinariness, indolence, and nondharmic actions for even a single moment.

---

3. The swallow is at first very careful, but later, when it sees no enemies, it flies directly to the nest, free from doubt and hesitation.

Although one may have understood the nature of emptiness, one should, with firm trust and confidence in the unfailing interdependence of cause and effect, refrain from belittling the importance of virtue and evil and train oneself in a combined view and behavior that accord with the words of the Victorious One.

In particular, since all the crucial points of the following bardos depend upon this present one, if one does not gain the power of acquaintance with practice while one has the freedom and leisure to do so during the bardo of this life, it will be too late for regret when, arriving at the point of death, one's time has run out. It would then be as Orgyen Rinpoche has said:

> Those who feel they have plenty of time get busy at the
> time of death.
> They then feel strong regret but it seems far too late.

It is therefore essential to train oneself in the bardos from this very moment on. Having practiced the oral instructions of the dharma-door, one has entered in accordance with one's particular destiny and inclination, and one should bring one's being to maturity and liberation. First of all, one should be sure to receive the stages of the ripening empowerments, be they condensed or elaborate.

Empowerment, as most of the masters of the present dark age perform the ritual, and the way it is received rarely accord with the tantras and the tradition of the vidyadhara forefathers. Many lamas perform the empowerments to amass wealth or for the sake of advantage and fame. Similarly, the disciples who are requesting empowerment simply seek protection against temporary harm such as sickness and demonic influences, prestige, or companionship, entertainment, or merely the satisfaction of their curiosity. Besides receiving the empowerment with these attitudes, they lack the substance of pure faith and seemingly cannot get even a fraction of the transmission of the nature of the empowerment. In short, where both master and disciple are involved in an empowerment of deceit, childish play, and parroting, there is obviously no means for ripening the person's mind.

In the meeting between a genuine vessel and elixir,[4] it doesn't really matter whether or not the superficial empowerment articles are placed on one's head. When the wisdom of the nature of the empowerment has dawned within one's being, that is the ultimate receiving of a true empowerment. For example, when Naropa awoke from fainting after being struck by the shoe in Tilopa's hand, he had realized the ultimate nature of empowerment. Or, like the learned Vairochana, who was given an apple by the great pandita Shri Singha and through that gesture of giving obtained the entire Dzogchen empowerment of awareness-display. There is also the story of Kyotön Sönam Lama, who conferred empowerment upon Machik Labdrön, as well as countless other examples in the life stories of the siddhas. The point is that one should not emphasize merely whether one has or has not received a certain empowerment, but rather should consider whether or not it has brought one to maturity.

Concerning the actual liberating instructions, by simply listing the teachings one has managed to request and receive, one's mind is surely not liberated. Ample proof exists that such a list can hardly cause one's kleshas to diminish even in the slightest or make one's ego-clinging and attachment decrease one bit. It is therefore generally important to exert oneself persistently in ways that would

---

4. Poetical expression for a qualified student and the authentic teachings.

allow one to correctly manifest the signs of the path of whatever teaching one is practicing or at least to gain some confidence in the meaning of its words.

Although there are indeed countless different instructions, in short, a practitioner who follows the profound path of the Six Doctrines or of the Path and Result should exert firm diligence in practicing tummo, the life-pillar of the path. By means of the trainings in the steady channels, moving winds, and arranged essences,[5] one should concentrate on the key points of the supreme path of the unconditioned coemergent wisdom, the union of bliss and emptiness. One should thus reach perfection by fully exerting oneself in ways that ripen the relative body composed of the elements into the nature of the pure rainbow body, and by accomplishing within this lifetime the united state of the two kayas that are of one taste in the nonarising space of dharmakaya, the ultimate essence of cognizance.

For a practitioner of Dzogchen, there is the outer Mind Section, the inner Space Section, the Secret Instruction Section and the innermost Unexcelled Section, as well as innumerable other classifications such as the Ati, Chiti and Yangti sections. In short, all the key points are included within these two: the Trekchö practice of awareness and emptiness and the Thögal practice of appearance and emptiness. No matter which system of Kama or Terma one enters, one should first receive complete instructions from an eminent master. In a secluded and unpopulated place one should then abandon the ninefold activities and make the separation of samsara and nirvana. If one then practices continuously day and night without mixing one's practice with any other activity for even a single moment, one will in this very body realize the dharmakaya state of Samantabhadra.

---

5. Also known as nadi, prana, and bindu.

People can be divided into nine categories of three higher, medium, and lower capacities. The highest of the superior type is liberated simultaneously with receiving the instructions, just as a knot in a snake is spontaneously released. This was the case of the great Vidyadhara Garab Dorje. The intermediate of the superior type is liberated after whatever occurs has dissolved into dharmata, just like snow falling on a lake. This was the case of those who attained the vajra-like form of the rainbow body, such as Manjushrimitra, Shri Singha, Vimalamitra, Padmakara, and others. The inferior of the superior type, like ice melting in water, must exert himself for a long time in the instructions, through which his deluded tendencies gradually decrease and his material body becomes liberated into the body of light. This was the case of Nyang Wen Tingdzin Sangpo, Chetsün Senge Wangchuk and the two Lobpön Nyangtön brothers, and others who attained khachö[6] without discarding their bodies.

In short, all those who reach perfect accomplishment within this lifetime through the profound teachings of Mahamudra, Dzogchen, Lamdre, Jordruk, Shije, Chöd,[7] and so forth, are liberated in this very body without having to go through the following bardos. That is the measure of having perfected the practice of the bardo of this life. These days however, there are extremely few examples of this kind no matter where one looks, whether in the Sarma or Nyingma school.

In any case, without falling under the power of distraction and indolence, one should concentrate exclusively on

---

6. The ability to depart for the realms of enlightened beings at the time of death without leaving a material body behind.

7. The teachings of the different lineages brought to Tibet by the great masters such as Guru Rinpoche, Vairochana, Vimalamitra, Marpa, Khyungpo Naljor, Atisha, Drogmi Lotsawa, Orgyenpa, Phadampa Sangye, and Machik Labdrön.

the main part of the practice, whether Mahamudra or Dzogchen, and apply the teachings on dream and luminosity in one's practice at night, the teachings on illusory body and bardo during all the breaks between practice periods, and mantra recitation and visualization of the guru and yidam at the beginning of the sessions, as well as dedication and aspirations at the end.

In brief, one should, in general, avoid dissipating one's three doors into ordinary confusion. In particular, from this very moment on, one should persistently keep in mind and familiarize oneself with all the practices of the following bardos. That is the essential point which alone is in harmony with the views of all the Sarma and Nyingma schools.

CONCLUDING VERSES

Having obtained the complete freedoms and riches, like a
  wish-fulfilling gem,
And having found a spiritual guide and profound
  teachings,
One is still distracted by the fascinating spectacle of
  samsara,
And thus attainment of the permanent goal is as rare as
  stars at daytime.

If enlightenment is not attained during this short time
While the sand castle body and small child's mind are
  together,
Although one lists one hundred things learned and
  understood,
This will not help in getting free from the ocean of
  samsara.

Remaining lazy while one has perfect freedom,
One will agonize with regret when the unavoidable Lord
  of Death arrives.
Staging one's own disaster like a madman drinking
  poison—
Thus the bardo of this life is manifest.

2
The Painful Bardo of Dying

THE EXPLANATION of the painful bardo of dying is also in three parts.

IDENTIFYING THE ESSENCE

The painful bardo of dying is the whole period from the time one is afflicted by the sickness that will cause one's death, whatever it may be, until the true luminosity of dharmata, the first bardo,[1] has arisen. The general dharma systems teach that the manifestation of this luminosity is included within the bardo of dying. At this point, however, I shall follow the Dzogchen teachings and describe only the bardo of dying. The luminous bardo of dharmata will be dealt with below.

The superior type of person (mentioned above) who is liberated in this lifetime need not go through the other bardos. The Dzogchen teachings state:

> The best yogins have four ways of dying. As space within and without mingle together when a vase breaks, so body and mind dissolve into the emptiness of dharmakaya. It is also like the flames that subside when firewood is consumed, or when a vidyadhara dies, filling the sky with a mass of light, or like a dakini

---

1. Calling the luminosity of dharmata the first bardo is according to the New Schools. In this book of four bardos, it is actually the third chapter.

whose death leaves no physical body behind. These are the superior ways of dying.

These four ways are free from the elaborations of the dissolution stages. Again, it has been taught:

> The mediocre yogins have three ways of dying. Dying like a small child, free from the reckoning of dying or not dying at the time of death. Dying like a wandering beggar, free from fear of circumstances. Dying like a lion, in unpeopled snow mountains, after having cut attachment to circumstances. These are all the middling ways of dying.

In these ways of dying one has the confidence of realization and does not depend upon being reminded.

DETAILED EXPLANATION OF THE GENERAL MANNER IN WHICH DYING TAKES PLACE

For inferior yogins and ordinary people there are two points:

1. Explaining how the outer elements, faculties, and sense-bases dissolve
2. Explaining how the inner gross and subtle thoughts dissolve

In addition, there is also explanation of the oral instructions on phowa.

HOW THE OUTER ELEMENTS DISSOLVE

In general, the body of a being is first formed by means of the five elements. Later, it also subsists by means of them, and finally, it perishes through their dissolution.

At the time of death, the wind of karma turns back upward, and as it controls all the winds, the nadi-knots of the five chakras fall apart and the five winds begin to disappear. Thereby the outer, inner, and secret elements dissolve into one another. The details of these dissolution stages can be found in the Dzogchen tantra *Rigpa Rangshar,*[2] but fearing the mass of words I shall not go into such extensive explanation here. Condensing the vital points according to what is common to the Sarma and Nyingma schools, I shall explain them as follows.

With the disappearance of the equal-abiding wind one is unable to digest food and, beginning with the extremities, heat is withdrawn from the body. The disappearance of the life-upholding wind makes one's mind unclear and confused. The disappearance of the downward-clearing wind makes one unable to defecate. The disappearance of the upward-moving wind makes one unable to swallow any food or drink and one becomes short of breath. With the disappearance of the pervading wind one loses the full use of the limbs and the veins begin to shrink.

The beginning of the destruction of the nadi-wheels is the disintegration of the nadi-wheel of the navel. After that, step by step, the disappearance of the supporting wind makes the earth element dissolve into the water element. The outer sign of that occurrence is the loss of physical strength; the neck cannot support the head, the legs cannot support the body, the hand cannot support a plate of food, the face takes on an ugly texture, dark stains collect on the teeth, and one cannot withhold the saliva and nasal mucus. After the outer signs, the inner signs are that the mind, extremely dull and obscured, draws one into complete depression. Holding back with the hands, tearing at clothing, crying "Lift me up!," one tries to look

---

2. *Rig pa rang shar chen po'i rgyud.* This text is found among the Hundred Thousand Nyingma Tantras *(Rnying ma rgyud 'bum),* published by H. H. Dilgo Khyentse Rinpoche.

up. At this point, the secret signs of luminosity manifest vaguely like a mirage.

Following that, when the nadi-wheel of the heart center is disintegrating, the disappearance of the radiance-producing wind makes the water element dissolve into the fire element. The outer signs of this are that the mouth and tongue dry up, the nostrils become drawn in, and the tongue is twisted and becomes inflexible. The inner signs are that one's mind feels hazy, nervous, and irritated. The secret sign is that experience becomes misty like smoke.

After that, the nadi-wheel of the throat disintegrates, and the disappearance of the refining wind forces the fire element to dissolve into the wind element. The outer signs of this are that the breath chills the mouth and nose, and the heat of one's body slips away, letting vapor stream forth, and the warmth withdraws from the extremities. The inner signs are that one's mind feels alternately clear and unclear. One hardly recognizes anything and cannot clearly perceive the outer appearances. Scintillating red lights like fireflies appear as the secret sign.

Then, due to the disintegration of the nadi-wheel of the secret place and the disappearance of the karmic wind of the kalpa, the wind element dissolves into consciousness. The outer signs of this are that the breath rattles, choked with long exhalations and difficult inhalations, and the eyes turn upward. The inner signs are that one is bewildered and has various visions. The evil-minded see the Lord of Death appear. Terrified, writhing in panic, faces contorted by fear, they cry out. Those with good karma, it is said, will see dakas and dakinis coming to welcome them, among many other virtuous visions. The secret sign that heralds this is like a flaming torch.

At the time that the five elements and the five primary winds have thus dissolved, the five subsidiary winds will also automatically disappear, and through this all the sense-faculties and sense-bases also gradually dissolve. Thus, the abilities of the sense-faculties of the eyes, ears, nose, tongue, and body degenerate and dissolve. As a result, one will not be able to perceive forms, sounds, odors, tastes, or textures. One will misapprehend them or become unable to distinguish their qualities.

After that, while consciousness dissolves in space the external breathing stops. At this point one's body color fades and dissipates, and there's only slight warmth at the heart. In texts such as *Liberating from the Dangerous Path of the Bardo,* everything up to this point comprises the "general signs of death." Here at this dividing point, it is said that some people can revive again when the cause is illness or an evil influence.

HOW THE INNER THOUGHTS DISSOLVE

From this point on, no one can turn back, having encountered the "special signs of death" of the dissolution stages of the gross and subtle thoughts. These are described in the *Kalachakra Root Tantra:*

> When those who have a body die,
> The nectar moon moves downward,
> The sun dust eclipse moves upward,
> And the consciousness has the nature of becoming.

According to this statement, when the eighty innate thoughts resulting from the three poisons cease, with the dissolution of appearance, increase, and attainment, the whiteness and so forth will manifest. It is not definite at this time which of the two, the whiteness or the redness, will manifest first. Here, however, I will expound upon this according to the Kalachakra teachings. That is to say, at the upper end of the central channel of all who have bodies, at the crown of the head, is the element obtained from the father, the relative and causal essence in the form of the white syllable HANG. The disappearing of the upper wind makes this element descend through the path of the central channel. In one's personal experience, whiteness appears like moonshine, and at the same time the thirty-three different thought states resulting from anger come to an end. They are as follows:

[1] Detachment, [2] medium and [3] intense,
[4] Mental engagement and [5] disengagement,
[6] Lesser sadness, [7] medium and [8] intense,
[9] Peace and [10] conceptualization,
[11] Fear and [12] medium fear and [13] intense fear,
[14] Craving, [15] medium craving, and [16] intense craving,
[17] Grasping, [18] nonvirtue, [19] hunger, and [20] thirst,
[21] Sensation, [22] medium sensation, and [23] intense sensation,
[24] Cognizing and [25] fixation-basis for cognizing,
[26] Discrimination and [27] conscience,
[28] Compassion, [29] love, [30] medium love, and [31] intense love,
[32] Attraction and [33] jealousy.

These are the thirty-three thought states. All of them will thus have ceased.

Following that, at the lower end of the central channel, the navel center, is the element obtained from one's mother, the red essence in the form of the A-stroke. The disappearance of the lower wind makes it move upward.

At this point one experiences a redness, and at the same time the forty thought states resulting from desire also come to an end. They are as follows:

[1] Desire and [2] clinging,
[3] Joy, [4] medium joy, and [5] intense joy,
[6] Rejoicing and [7] deep respect,
[8] Amazement, [9] satisfaction, [10] sensual excitement, and [11] embracing,
[12] Kissing, [13] sucking, and [14] clasping,
[15] Vigor, [16] pride, and [17] engagement,
[18] Accompanying, [19] strength, and [20] delight,
[21] Lesser, [22] medium, and [23] intense joining in bliss,
[24] Haughtiness and [25] flirtation,
[26] Hostility, [27] virtue, and [28] lucidity,
[29] Truth, [30] untruth, and [31] understanding,
[32] Grasping, [33] generosity, [34] encouragement, and [35] courage,
[36] Shamelessness, [37] retention, and [38] viciousness,
[39] Unruliness and [40] deceitfulness.

All of these will thus have ceased.

Following that, the cognizance moved by the pervading wind dissolves within the meeting of the white and red bodhicittas, and at this point one experiences a blackness, and the seven thought states resulting from delusion also are brought to an end. They are as follows:

[1] The moment of medium desire,
[2] Forgetfulness, [3] confusion, and [4] being stunned,
[5] Weariness, [6] laziness, and [7] doubt.

These were the seven. All of these will thus have ceased.

It is said that some people experience the intense suffering of the interruption of life. Other people at this point, when the dissolution stages have ceased, experience the so-called space dissolving in luminosity, owing to the pure essences of the channels, winds, elements, and mind having gathered in the heart center. Thus, the basic luminosity of the first bardo³ appears to even the tiniest insect.

EXPLANATION OF HOW TO PRACTICE THESE BARDO STATES

In general, one should constantly keep in mind the impermanence of all compounded things: in particular that the time of one's death is uncertain, and especially that at the time of dying nothing whatsoever can help one, except the oral instructions from one's master. If one does not remember this and practice, one will surely arrive at death regretful, still trying to comprehend various categories of teachings or struggling in the pursuit of pleasure, food, and clothing. The *Chedu Jöpe Tsom* states:

> All people feel attachment to their possessions—
> To children, cattle, and wealth;
> "That I have done, now I do this.
> When this has been done, I will then do that."
> While people are thus being fooled by distractions,
> They depart, snapped away by the Lord of Death.

In this and other ways, this has been extensively taught in the sutras, tantras, and treatises, as well as in the spiritual songs of the learned and accomplished masters.

Similarly, many people, failing to condense their dharma practice to the essential, discover when in need that they have been fooling themselves with the sciences,⁴ studies, and reflections.

---

3. This is the empty luminosity, the naked nature of mind.
4. Grammar, debate, healing, and craftsmanship.

In particular, when the time to die comes, one should completely cast away worries about what needs to be done or accomplished, disregard whatever unfinished tasks remain, whether religious or secular, and give up all kinds of mental activity of attachment or aggression towards anyone, be they friends or relatives, spouse or intimates, high or low. Holding nothing back, abandon totally as offerings or charity all types of material things and belongings: from the biggest shrine objects of body, speech, and mind, down to the smallest needle and thread. The most vital point is to free oneself from any mental residue of concern, even as much as a hair's-breadth, toward any object of attachment. So make up your mind decisively.

One's thought at the time of death is extremely strong, so actually or mentally make confession and retake your vows against all kinds of even the most subtle faults or downfalls, noticed or unnoticed, in your precepts and samayas.[5] Even if your master is physically present, you should still visualize the objects of refuge and the guru yoga and with concentration receive the empowerments and vows. It is most excellent if you also have a companion with pure samayas and the same teachings who knows how to remind you of the oral instructions.

Furthermore, it is most important to send ordinary friends and relatives, along with their cries and lamentations, outside of one's retreat boundary, as they are but causes for generating attachment or aggression. As explained previously, it is best to follow the path of the mountain deer, which, in dying, cuts off the complexities of companionship.

The explanation of the dissolution stages is just an

---

5. These refer to the hinayana vows of individual liberation, the mahayana trainings of a bodhisattva, and the samayas/commitments in vajrayana practice.

indication of how they occur for people in general. Oth-erwise, sequences of dissolution vary according to the differences of each person's individual channels, winds, and essences, as well as the unpredictable occurrences of the individual's sickness, evil influences, or the power of circumstances. For some people it happens that the stages dissolve together all at once, so it is impossible to make a definite generalization. In any case, it is essential to mem-orize and familiarize oneself with the sequences in which all the outer, inner, and secret signs manifest.

When the time for dying actually arrives, the body, at best, should be sitting upright. If one is unable to do so, one should lie on the right shoulder and assume the manner of a sleeping lion. One should concentrate on whichever practice one has been familiar with. Thus, one who has put emphasis on the self-cognizant mindfulness of empty luminosity, as in the practice of Mahamudra, in the Trekchö aspect of Dzogchen, in Shije, or in other teachings, should simply relax into the continuity of the dharmata nature during all the dissolution stages, which-ever occur. If one concentrates on just not wandering elsewhere or simply not being confused, one need not do anything else until reaching the basic luminosity. Having arrived there, liberation is attained without any hardship.

Otherwise, if one has trained in Jordruk or in the luminosity of light and darkness according to the Thögal aspect of Dzogchen, when the four elements dissolve one should confidently resolve that the gradual manifestations, such as the secret signs of smoke or mirage, are all nothing but the luminous dharmakaya manifestation of self-cogni-zance, and then exert oneself one-pointedly in the practice of the spontaneously present wisdom of luminous empti-ness.

Also, if one has been acquainted with the instructions of

the profound path of Mahamudra of bliss and emptiness according to Lamdre or Chödruk, one should in accordance with these teachings recognize the individual dissolution stages of mind and prana for each of the nadiwheels. In particular, when the whiteness manifests, one should recognize it as the luminosity of appearance and thereby realize the meaning of the practice of samayamudra and the wisdom of joy. Similarly, when the redness manifests, one should recognize it as the experience of increase and recollect the wisdom of the karma-mudra.

When the blackness manifests, one should rest evenly in the experience of attainment, the nature of the dharmamudra, and the wisdom of absence of joy or special joy. Mingle the pain of the interruption of life, whatever happens, with the practice and make sure not to be interrupted by any other negative frame of mind until the innate[6] has manifested.

Moreover, if one does not possess such experience or realization, one should then concentrate on the devotion of the guru yoga of blessings. That is to say, in the beginning when the earth element has dissolved and the luminosity of mirage manifests, one should visualize the master in one's heart center, generate one-pointed devotion toward him, and make mental supplications. When the water element has dissolved and the smokelike luminosity manifests, one should visualize the master in the navel center. When the fire element has dissolved and the firefly luminosity manifests, one should visualize the master in the forehead. When the wind element has dissolved and the torchlike luminosity manifests, it is taught that especially at this point one should concentrate on the guruphowa of supreme recollection.

---

6. Synonymous with the basic luminosity of dharmakaya.

PHOWA PRACTICE

Now, the associated explanation on phowa has three points: the different types of individuals, the time for phowa, and the actual phowa practice.

THE DIFFERENT TYPES OF INDIVIDUALS

The foremost practitioners will attain complete realization of the meaning of Mahamudra or Dzogchen within this very lifetime. Or if not, they will possess the confidence of liberation simultaneously with the last exhalation of breath. Such people have no need to apply an additional instruction on phowa. Nor do they need to have someone come to perform phowa for them. However, in order to guide other disciples, they may appear to be performing in the manner of phowa. Numerous masters have done this, for example Acharya Nagarjuna in India. Similarly, in Tibet, Lord Marpa, on the verge of passing into nirvana, transformed his consort Dagmema into a sphere of light and dissolved her into his heart center. Straightening his body, he said, "Sons, if you do phowa, do it like this!" Then a sphere of five-colored light the size of an egg ascended into the sky from a crack at the crown of his head. The siddha Melong Dorje as well, having finished singing a spiritual song of legacy amid a feast gathering, sent a white light the size of a cooking pot up in the air from the crown of his head. Growing bigger and bigger, it filled the sky with rainbows, lights, and circles.

A great many actions like these have indeed been performed by the innummerable siddhas and great beings of both the Sarma and Nyingma schools. Although these displays are labeled *phowa,* they do not in fact differ much from the rainbow body.

Moreover, phowa is said to be ineffective when performed by certain people who have violated the root samayas. Why is that? It is because the phowa teaching depends upon blessings and, since blessings depend upon the master, one cannot receive the blessings if one's samayas have been damaged at the root and not mended through confession. Thus phowa will be ineffective. It is, however, said in the *Tantra of the Four Vajra Seats:*

> Although one has performed the five misdeeds with
> immediate result
> One can be liberated through this path
> And will thus not be tainted by wrongdoing.

One may think that this is so, but this outcome occurs only for those who, although they initially committed wrongs, gain liberation after again engaging in practice. Furthermore, the verse is intended to mean that even a sinful person can be liberated through phowa if he has faith and has not violated the samaya to his vajra master.

THE TIME FOR PHOWA

It is still possible to come back to life during the dissolution of the gross outer elements. If phowa is performed for a person too early, there is the risk of creating the cause for a negative state of mind, such as hatred. A tantra says:

> Phowa should be done when the time has come.
> If it is untimely, one will be killing all the deities.[7]

For this reason, right timing is of vital importance. The time for visualizing the phowa is after all the elements, as explained above, have dissolved and the outer breathing has ceased, following which the whiteness manifests as the sign that the inner experience of appearance has dissolved.

---

7. This remark refers to the divinities inherent in one's body.

39

The time for actually performing the phowa is when the redness manifests as the sign that increase has dissolved. This is when sinners have the fearful vision of the Lord of Death, while those with pure karma see scenes of being welcomed by dakas and dakinis.

THE ACTUAL INSTRUCTION IN PHOWA

This instruction has two parts: training and application.

TRAINING IN PHOWA

First of all, training is of great importance. The numerous methods of practice have been condensed into five kinds: dharmakaya phowa free from reference point, sambhogakaya phowa of unity, nirmanakaya phowa of training, guru phowa of blessings, and the unmistaken phowa of khachö.

First let us discuss the meaning of the dharmakaya phowa. As previously explained, when one has attained stability in practices such as Mahamudra or Dzogchen, one need not engage in any additional training. In this context, according to the system of the Dzogchen Nyingthig,[8] the details of the teaching are as follows. When self-awareness, also called the lamp of self-existing knowledge, passes through the path of the lamp of the white and smooth channel and emerges through the gate of the far-reaching water lamp, there is the symbolic act of phowa into the field, the lamp of pure space. So, if one has trained in these teachings, one should practice like that. According to the profound Chödruk, the so-called innate phowa of the natural state is also simply the dharmakaya phowa itself.

Second, the sambhogakaya phowa of unity is the do-

8. See Appendix: The Dzogchen Tantras.

main of persons who have attained mastery over the perfect development stage or, according to Chödruk, have realization in the practice of the pure illusory body. In brief, both dharmakaya phowa and sambhogakaya phowa are only for those who in this life have fully trained in the stages of completion and development, through which they will effortlessly become accomplished whenever the time of death arrives; they are not for ordinary people. The sambhogakaya includes also the ultimate phowa of the great secret.

Third, for the nirmanakaya phowa of training, or the magical phowa of vivid presence, it is extremely important that one begin training immediately from this time on. It doesn't matter which tantra one uses as an instruction manual or whether one follows a specific teaching on phowa. In any case, one should receive the teaching from a master possessing experience and blessings and then train until the signs appear. Preceded by refuge and bodhicitta, the main part is as follows.

Concentrate one-pointedly on the key point of body posture for how to sit, the key point of prana for ejecting and entering, and the key point of visualization for conjuring and transformation. Within the state of the development stage, with your body as any suitable yidam, close the eight doors to samsara and visualize the hollowness of the central channel inside your empty body, which is a manifest emptiness. Meditate upon Amitabha (or whichever supreme deity you have devotion to) as being above the window of the brahma opening.[9] Train in sending the traveler—essence of prana-mind in the form of a deity, seed-syllable, symbolic attribute, or sphere of light—up and down through the path of the central channel. At the

---

9. The crown of one's head, about eight fingers above the hairline.

end of the session, practice the oral instructions on life extension.

In short, one should train exactly according to the text of the particular system that one is following. If one happens to need additional details or alterations, one should rely totally on one's teacher and practice until the signs show.

Fourth, for the guru phowa of blessings, one should visualize the deity above the crown of the head as being one's guru. Apart from that, the teachings are generally the same as the nirmanakaya phowa above. It is essential, for this practice in particular, to faithfully regard one's master as a buddha in person.

Fifth, the khachö phowa means cultivating pure realms. For this one must be a person trained in the emanations and transformations of dream practice. The instructions are identical with those on how to be confirmed with rebirth in a natural nirmanakaya realm as taught in the Dzogchen teachings.

APPLICATION OF PHOWA

Whichever type of phowa one practices, one should have perfect and one-pointed trust in the particular objective one aims at, without falling prey to disturbing emotions such as attachment to the things of this life or the three poisons. Since even the slightest unwholesome frame of mind will be a hindrance to phowa, when the time of death arrives one should not be governed by negative thoughts even for a single instant, but should shoot to the target of one's focus without a single doubt. Like the arrow released by a skilled archer, one should be beyond return. In that way, like a boat steered by oars or a horse directed by the bit, one will accomplish whatever is one's purpose.

People say, "Phowa, phowa," but the important point is that, having recognized one's flawless awareness, one should apply the key points of the oral instructions and dissolve into dharmadhatu, without going astray on a mistaken path. So a person who has made aspirations for many lifetimes, who has some gathering of the two accumulations, and furthermore who in this life does not pervert his devotion to the teaching and the master of the vajra vehicle of secret mantra and is free from violations of his samayas, will indeed easily attain realization. This seems, however, hardly to be the case for just anyone. In order for a great sinner to instantly attain enlightenment, it is evident that the right coincidences, as explained above must come together. Therefore, a most vital point is to acquaint oneself with the oral instructions and arrange the right coincidences now, while one has the freedom and time.

CONCLUDING VERSES

Though the rain of the profound meaning of the sutra and
    tantra teachings showers down
From the compassion of the noble victorious ones and
    their sons,
It is difficult for a single sprout of a ripened and freed
    mind
To grow forth in sentient beings whose minds are
    confused, attached and grasping.

Governed this entire life by nondharmic actions,
The truly needed sacred dharma is cast away, to dissipate.
At the time of death, when the mirror of deep regret
Reflects one's very face, it will be too late.

Of all those who are bright-minded and shrewd in human
    affairs
And of those who are learned in mere words and theories,
When faced with the onset of a fatal sickness,
Who do you think will risk to reap the loss?

3
The Luminous Bardo of Dharmata

THE EXPLANATION OF the nature of the luminous bardo of dharmata has three parts:

1. Identifying its essence
2. Elucidating its manner of manifesting
3. Telling how to apply the oral instructions

IDENTIFYING THE ESSENCE

First, what is the essence of this bardo? After all the previously mentioned dissolution stages are finished, the prana-mind will dissolve between the white and red pure essences, the A and HANG, union of means and knowledge. Because of this coincidence, the dharmakaya of primordial luminosity, the noncomplex, unfabricated, coemergent wisdom of great bliss, will definitely manifest.

Among the many names for this coemergent wisdom, the Causal Vehicles call it ultimate transcendent knowledge. The Madhyamika followers call it ultimate truth. In Mahamudra it is called recognition within nonthought. The followers of the Mind Section of Dzogchen call it awareness resuming its essence. In all the Secret Cycles of Luminosity it is called the welcoming light of spontaneous presence. The followers of the Profound Path call it mahamudra of coemergent wisdom. But the general teachings common to all systems know it as the luminosity of the first bardo.

DETAILED EXPLANATION OF ITS MANNER OF MANIFESTATION

This explanation has two parts: the general and the particular.

GENERAL EXPLANATION

Most tantras call the series of the "mirage" and so forth, as explained above, the apparent luminosity, whereas the ground luminosity, after the dissolution stages are completed, is called the nonapparent luminosity, or empty luminosity. Some call the manifestation modes of "appearance, increase, and attainment" the sign luminosity, and this main part[1] itself is called the true luminosity. This is described in the *Nyime Namgyal:*

> At first, the mirage will be seen,
> Endowed with fivefold rays of light.
> Second, it is like the moon.
> Third, it is like the sun.
> Fourth, it is like darkness.

These embody the sign luminosities, after which:

> Fifth, like the sky free from clouds,
> Nonthought dawns free from center or periphery.

That is the true luminosity itself.

Why are these called sign luminosities? It is because at first, the mirage and the other [visions] are the signs of the five sense consciousnesses dissolving into the all-ground. Similarly, the whiteness signals that the afflicted mind consciousness is dissolving into the all-ground, the redness that mind consciousness is dissolving, and the blackness that the ignorant aspect of the all-ground is dissolving into

---

1. The main part, here, is the basic nature of mind, laid bare after the preliminary stages of appearance, increase, and attainment.

itself. When everything has dissolved into the ultimate dharmadhatu, then the immaculate dharmakaya wisdom will manifest.

Now follows the reason why the ground luminosity manifests here in such a way. The sugatagarbha is present within all sentient beings and pervades them from the beginning. Obscured by coemergent ignorance, or the ignorant aspect of the all-ground, the wisdom present in oneself stands unrecognized, and therefore each being is continually submerged in confusion. Since this obscuration dissolves in itself for a short while at the time of the dissolution stages, wisdom then manifests nakedly, appearing even to ordinary people. They fail to recognize it, and the habitual pattern of obscuration repeats itself. Again and again, people continue to the following rebirth, and samsaric existence endures as an unbroken chain.

For practitioners well acquainted with the main points of these instructions, the mother luminosity, which is the self-manifest original nature, and the child luminosity, what has been practiced as the path, will mingle inseparably together. They meet as old friends, or like a river flowing into the ocean. For this reason liberation is easy.

The Sarma Schools of Secret Mantra teach that in the pure dharmadhatu palace of ultimate Akanishta dwells the teacher endowed with the seven aspects of union: the great Vajradhara, the sovereign of the equal taste of space and wisdom.

The Nyingma system teaches that in the All-pervading Realm of the Great Expanse, the two—the "mind and doer" Samantabhadra, king of self-cognizance, and the "mental object and deed" Samantabhadri, the utterly pure nature of space—dwell as the indivisible great bliss, the essence of primordial purity in the unchanging fourth time of equality.

In short, all the introductory chapters of the profound tantras of secret mantra speak exclusively of this nature as a description of divinities. The meaning is, however, indeed difficult for narrow-minded people and intellectuals to comprehend.

Concerning this point, the essential meaning with which I have become familiar is in complete agreement with the vajra verses, advice, and quotations of all the great masters. At this point, all the tantras of the Sarma and Nyingma schools and all the vidyadharas and siddhas share the same view that this ground luminosity is certainly the liberation-basis of the ultimate dharmakaya essence.

The testament of Lord Jonangpa, however, states: "That which some other lamas believe to be 'luminosity' is merely attachment to the occurrence of a small portion of a blissful feeling, due to prana entering the central channel of a person who has attained a minor degree of stability in shamatha. This is called 'cave luminosity' and should not be considered the real luminosity." Although this statement is quite famous, it was most likely meant for some special purpose. Otherwise, all the dharma traditions seem to have an identical view on this point.

Moreover, since most people fail to recognize the ground luminosity, even though it manifests for them, or they are not sufficiently acquainted with it even if they recognize it, they are not able to remain in its continuity. Apart from that, there is no doubt that it is the true ground of liberation. This is described in the *Dzogchen Senge Tsaldzog Tantra;*[2]

---

2. One of the seventeen tantras of the Instruction Section of Dzogchen.

The nature of the mind of all buddhas
Pervades all sentient beings naturally from the beginning.
When this secret awareness is manifest in the field [of
  experience],
It manifests five lights, in the manner of mother and child
  meeting.

When the child manifestations dissolve into the mother,
All displays of dualistic mind are cleared away.
The doubt of confused thoughts and statements is cut,
And the illumination of the wisdom sunlight
Completely disperses all conceptual things.

By the power of being free from the doubt of conceptual
  thinking,
Awareness wisdom will be strengthened
And will rest accordingly in the state of nonthought.
The unmanifest wisdom will perceive everything.

When the fruit of secret mantra has fully ripened,
Awareness wisdom cannot help but manifest.
At that time, one's awareness having awakened,
The essence of occurring perceptions is utterly pure.

The nature of wisdom devoid of words is experienced,
And the genuine manifestations of secret mantra are seen.
When one is not engaging in cognition of "is" and "is
  not,"
Samadhi will be attained in five days.

The *Union of Sun and Moon Tantra*[3] states:

Therefore, being untainted, it is sufficient.
Self-occurring self-liberation, the expanse of nonarising.
Spontaneous presence dissolves into the space of
  primordial purity,
Free from the extremes of hope and fear.
The limits of both cause and effect having ceased,
Space and awareness, without duality, are freed into
  primordial purity,

---

3. The name of one of the eighteen tantras of the Instruction Section
of Dzogchen.

The spontaneous great perfection of nonaction.

Moreover, according to the *Kalachakra Root Tantra:*

When recognizing this luminosity,
One will definitely, with no intermediate state,
Be liberated from all sufferings and miseries.

Also, it is stated in the *Nyime Namgyal:*[4]

The person who has recognized this luminosity
Will not see the city of the bardo.
The appearance of rupakaya for the benefit of others will
    manifest
Like the analogy of a wishfulfilling jewel.

There being countless such statements, one should feel
no doubt.

PARTICULAR EXPLANATION

Now that I have explained the general systems, there is
a further twofold division: the dharmakaya luminosity of
primordial purity and the sambhogakaya luminosity according to the systems of the Instruction Section of
Dzogchen and the Innermost Unexcelled Cycle of Nyingthig.

The first division is exactly the ground luminosity of
the natural state, which manifests like a pure and cloudless
sky. So, if one recognizes one's nature here, in that very
recognition one will attain enlightenment in the great
original state of primordial purity and will therefore be
free from the later residual manifestations.

If, however, one is only slightly acquainted with this
state and is thus unable to be liberated, the inner breath
will cease and the red element will emerge from the right
nostril in the form of blood or lymph and the white

---

4. A tantric text belonging to the New Schools.

element will emerge from the secret path. At the same time, awareness, like a spark fading, will emerge from any of the apertures, such as the eyes, and the bardo of dharmata will manifest. The period up to that point is called the dharmakaya luminosity of primordial purity.

If one is not liberated at this point, then, at the end of space dissolving in luminosity, the luminosity dissolving in unity occurs. At this instant the wrathful heruka deities will reveal themselves in all their attires and attributes, with numerous heads, wearing various ornaments, filling the entire world. The spontaneous sound of dharmata will roar like thousands of thunderclaps, and colors and lights will ignite like a hailstorm of weapons.

Amid this immense terror, without recognizing one's essence, one now becomes panic-stricken and faints. When one has regained consciousness, all the above has completely vanished, and the peaceful deities gradually manifest.

Then all perceived objects, such as earth, stones, mountains, and rocks, totally devoid of materiality, are of the nature of rainbow light, completely clear and shining. Vast and free from obstruction, brilliant and magnificent, they manifest with a nature that totally transcends all limitations. At this point one will think that one has the body of one's former life. Completely pervading space in all directions, above and below, countless rainbow lights in the form of five-colored spheres manifest, and within each of them are the innumerable peaceful deities of vajradhatu, such as the five families of victorious ones and the male and female bodhisattvas, all with wonderful expressions and attire captivating to behold. Extremely fine rays of light extend from each of their heart centers and connect to one's own. All of these manifestations are completely ordered. From the rays connected to one's heart, countless fine spheres will also be seen to emanate. Later, one experiences all of these forms dissolving into oneself.

After that, unity dissolving into wisdom appears. From one's heart center and into the space above, blue, white, yellow, and red lights shine forth, one above the other, like extended banners. Each is adorned with spheres of light in its corresponding color, which is again decorated with five smaller spheres. Like a parasol of peacock feathers, they appear splendidly above oneself, in the full five colors. All this is called the inner path of Vajrasattva. It is the light path of the four wisdoms combined. The green light path does not appear, owing to the lack of all-accomplishing wisdom, because one has not perfected the power of practice.

Next appears the wisdom dissolving into the vidyadhara of spontaneous presence. The previously mentioned manifestations of light dissolve into the parasollike five lights above. Next, everywhere above these personal phenomena, the dharmakaya display will manifest like a cloudless sky, symbolizing the awareness and emptiness of primordial purity. In between will manifest the rupakaya of spontaneous presence, the realms of the peaceful and wrathful ones, as well as the various natural nirmanakaya realms. Below will appear scenes of the impure worlds of the six classes of beings. All of this manifests simultaneously with vivid clarity, like an image appearing in a mirror.

At this point, it is the nature of things that the person will automatically have the five superknowledges, the six recollections, and perfect recall, as well as continuous samadhi. Moreover, it is also taught that innumerable dharma teachings, previously known as well as unknown, will arise within one's mind.

In short, liberation is assured if one remembers at this appropriate time the vital points of the oral instructions, whichever have been taught, and puts them into practice. But if the power of one's practice is feeble and one is not liberated, one will for a while see the dream appearances of the bardo of becoming and then doubtlessly pass on to a natural nirmanakaya realm. Having swiftly traversed all the paths and bhumis, it is taught that one will attain enlightenment.

HOW TO BRING THE BARDO OF DHARMATA INTO THE PATH

What is the duration from the initial bardo of dying until this point? It seems, because of the words used and the intervals and the duration of all that transpires, that these bardo stages appear for a long time, whereas in fact they do not last very long. In the first place, given the different nadi constitutions and circumstances of individuals and their illnesses, generalizing about the outer and inner dissolution stages is indeed impossible. Most often, however, stages quickly pass.

In particular, it is taught that the whiteness, redness, and blackness last no longer than one instant of completed action. When, after that, the dharmakaya luminosity of death, the coemergent wisdom, dawns, it does not usually last longer than a finger snap for ordinary people who have not practiced. Some can stay for the "duration of a meal." Also, people who have practiced slightly can remain for as long as they once could retain stability in the practice of meditation. That is called a "meditation day." It is taught that one remains in this luminosity for between one and five such days.

Practitioners possessing the confidence of realization are able to remain in composure in that state of luminosity for as long as they wish. At the end, for such people, the wisdom wind will dispatch awareness through the crown of the head and they will attain the "great upper directness." This is indicated by the white bodhicitta appearing at the crown of the head or the left nostril when the vital point of the wisdom wind moves in the left channel. During a successful phowa, the bodhicitta appears in this way. Without this sign, claims to a successful phowa are doubtful.

Some learned and accomplished masters, such as Jamyang Palden Sangpo, have stated that those who remain for a long time before their consciousness leaves the body are not necessarily resting in perfect meditation, as there are some people who remain because of attachment to their bodies.

In any case, for people of any of the three capacities, it is totally inappropriate to cremate and perform purification rituals for the body as long as the white and red essences have not emerged from either above or below. Why is this? The cremation will be an obstacle for those remaining in meditation, and an ordinary person attached to his body will be burned alive.

Now, as for the luminosity manifestations of spontaneous presence according to Dzogchen, those who are only slightly advanced in practice will experience them for one to five meditation days, corresponding to their degree of familiarity. For those who are not so acquainted, they will last no longer than an instant of completed action and are therefore difficult to recognize. Some, by failing to recognize the sounds, colors, and lights as their own personal experience, become terrified and faint.

Having described the additional points, here is the main part of the chapter.

The supreme method for recognizing the ground luminosity of the first bardo and attaining liberation is to become fully resolved about the mind right now in the bardo of the present life, and then to exclusively concentrate, beyond meditation and distraction, on continuous practice of the ultimate nature of ordinary mind, the unfabricated and natural state of dharmakaya. Knowing how to maintain it, unspoiled by the obstacles of defects or defilements, mental constructs and fabrications, is crucial not only in the first bardo but at all times. It is the ultimate essence and supreme extract of all the sutras, tantras, and oral instructions. Since all the 84,000 teachings are contained and complete within this, it is the Great Perfection [Dzogchen]. Since nothing departs from the three kayas, it is the Great Seal [Mahamudra]. Since it transcends intellectual constructs, it is Transcendent Knowledge [Prajnaparamita]. Free from all extremes, it is the Middle Way [Madhyamika]. Actualizing the result of the supreme path, it is Path and Fruition [Lamdre]. Since it naturally pacifies disturbing emotions, it is the Pacifier [Shije]. Since it cuts clinging and fixation to dualistic experience at their root, it is the Cutting [Chöyul]. Since it in actuality unites one with the state of enlightenment, it is the Six Unions [Jordruk]. Since it purifies ignorance and confused thinking, it is Mind Training [Lojong]. In short, all the innumerable kinds of profound teachings converge here at exactly this vital point. So, by not vigorously concentrating on this true meaning, one's intellectual pursuit of numerous plans will prove ineffective at the time of need. This is described in the *Künje Gyalpo Tantra*:[5]

---

5. A tantra belonging to the Mind Section of Dzogchen. It is included in the *Kangyur, sNying rgyud*, Vol. Ka.

When you realize the suchness of your mind,
The buddha will not linger among mere words.
So the highest yoga is attained right now.
For the undestined ones of inferior fortune,
Even were the hidden revealed, they would not understand,
Just as someone wishing for a precious jewel
Will not gain it from polishing a piece of wood.

Thus, it is essential to exert oneself in the unmistaken nature right now.

In particular, one should also apply oneself assiduously to the steps of training in luminosity as they occur in texts such as the *Six Doctrines, Liberation through Hearing,* and so forth. When one attains stability in the luminosity of realization during the state of deep sleep, recognizing the ground luminosity at this point in the bardo of dharmata will not be difficult.

Know, then, that if one can practice virtue while, sleeping, one can recognize the first luminosity. This differentiates between actually remaining in meditation and just remaining in the body out of attachment. When someone appears to be genuinely remaining in meditation, one who knows how can give the reminding-instruction. Complex practices such as phowa cannot be performed with concepts. In short, it is evident that for such realized people there is no need to depend upon deliberate ceremonies such as purification rituals or name-burning.

As for the pointing out of the apparent luminosity, the person who is acquainted with such practices as the five-fold Path of Means, Jordruk, and so forth, should recognize that whatever appears—such as the mirage, whiteness, and other signs—is all simply a manifestation of dharmakaya, one's self-cognizance. For practitioners of Thögal according to Dzogchen it is essential to trust that whatever appears, such as the sounds, colors, and lights, the peaceful and wrathful deities, the bindus, light rays, light paths, and pure realms—all are nothing other than one's natural manifestation, and then rest evenly in the state of having resolved that. To be able to do this, one should certainly practice right now in becoming certain about the ground nature of Trekchö, and in concentrating on the pointing out instructions of the path of Thögal.

These days it seems that dharma practitioners with only rough understanding are mistaking the two names Bön and Nyingma. They can therefore not be included among dharma followers. In particular, concerning the profound teachings of Dzogchen, many, such as Garab Dorje, Jampal Shenyen, Shri Singha, and the Twenty-five Panditas, indeed attained the body of light. They all practiced in the manner of keeping secrecy and did not, like us Tibetans, engage in salesmanship, pursuing profit, fame, and gain. For this reason they were not so famous.

Only a few volumes of the six million tantras, for the most part kept in the realms of the wisdom dakinis and vidyadharas, are present in this human world. Here in Tibet, at the time of the Early Spread of the Teachings, numerous fortunate people were liberated into the body of light through the kindness of Orgyen, Vimalamitra, and Vairochana.

Although today the many Oral Lineages and Treasure Lineages are still available, some teachers, headed by Go Lhatse and Drigung Paldzin, claim that Dzogchen as it was in India does not exist today, and they therefore try to prove that it is not a genuine teaching or maintain that it is the Hashang view. Criticizing these teachings as merely Tibetan compositions carries the danger of harming the faithful. Because they have not even glanced at these teachings in the Kangyur, Gyübum, or other scriptures, most people shun the teachings of the Three Yogas, including

Dzogchen, as if seeing the corpse of a man who died of the plague.

Those who claim to follow the Nyingma tradition busy their minds with protections, exorcism, and casting spells, in order to feed their attendants, wives, and children. They pursue village rituals for gain. Making drinking their main practice, they never have a chance to hear the key points of Dzogchen, nor even a fraction of them. By these divergent practices they will surely not attain the body of light within one lifetime or be liberated in the first bardo. It is evident that they have passed up the opportunity to have the intention, much less the understanding, to recognize the bardo of dharmata. What Gyalwa Yang Gönpa said is only too true: "It doesn't help that the teachings are Dzogchen, it is the person who needs to be Dzogchen."

Having in all honesty expressed these points about the way the manifestations appear, I turn to the actual topic of this chapter.

According to Dzogchen roots texts, Trekchö has these three points:[6] recognizing one's essence, deciding on one thing, and gaining confidence in liberation. Thögal has the various points, after resolving the nature of the six lamps, of laying the basis on the threefold motionlessness, keeping the measure of the threefold remaining, planting the stake of the threefold attainment, and showing the degree of liberation through the fourfold confidence.

When one does not let these and other points remain as mere rhetoric, but applies their meaning to one's being, one will perfect the four visions, and, at best, liberate the physical body into the unconditioned body of light. As the next best, one will attain stability in the ground

---

6. Also known as Garab Dorje's *Three Words Striking the Vital Point.*

luminosity just as the space within and outside a vase mingle together when the vase breaks, and thus, just like a lion emerging from the enclosure of the womb or a garuda leaving the enclosure of the eggshell, one's mind attains dharmakaya simultaneously with being freed from the enclosure of the physical body of karmic ripening. As the third best, when the spontaneously present luminosity of the rupakayas manifest in the bardo of dharmata, it is of utmost importance to possess the key point of knowing how to enter at the time of luminosity dissolving into union, the key point of liberated body at the time of union dissolving into wisdom, and the key point of recognizing the perfection at the time of wisdom dissolving into the vidyadhara level of spontaneous presence.

Concerning this time of spontaneous presence, a tantra states:

> As for how the spontaneously present awareness manifests,
> It manifests as eight kinds of gates.

According to this statement, the expression of awareness itself is manifest as compassion, manifest as light, manifest as bodies, manifest as wisdom, manifest as nonduality, manifest as freedom from extremes, manifest as the impure gate of samsara, and manifest as the pure gate of wisdom. When these gates are embraced by the oral instructions, there will also be eight modes of dissolution.

By compassion dissolving, samsaric sentient beings are liberated as personal experience and thus there is not even a hint of confusion. Likewise, by the light dissolving, there is one taste as dharmadhatu, which is not made of conceptual colors and not divided into families. By the bodies dissolving, there is purity as complete as the essence that transcends the elaborations of heads and arms. By the wisdom dissolving, the mother and child of dharmata mingle together. By nonduality dissolving, the three-thousandfold world system is liberated into the essence itself. By the freedom from extremes dissolving, the referential objects are exhausted. By the gate of samsara dissolving, one is free from the deluded object of a birth place. By the pure gate of wisdom dissolving into the essence body, one is enlightened in the great primordial purity, the exhaustion of phenomena beyond concepts.

The *Great Vastness of Space Tantra*[7] states:

> As long as this material body has not been abandoned,
> The enlightened qualities will not manifest.
> As, for instance, a garuda birdling within its egg
> May have developed its full wing feathers,
> But it cannot fly before hatching.
> The egg breaking open and the ability to fly then occur
>   simultaneously.
> Similarly, the qualities of buddhahood also
> Are not manifest at present but are veiled by the body.
> As soon as the body of karmic ripening is discarded,
> The enlightened qualities will be manifest.

The *Gongpa Thigdeb* also states:

> If one possesses the great confidence of realization,
> Just as a lion reaches far in one leap,
> Through the great openness of wisdom
> There will be no bardo and, in one instant,
> One will attain enlightenment in the Precious Sphere.

As for the measure of liberation, the *Union of Sun and Moon Tantra* says:

> There are three levels of capacity: Those of foremost capacity will be liberated in three instants. The mediocre can be liberated in five meditation days or will definitely attain stability in twenty-one instants. Those of the

---

7. *Nam mkha' klong yangs chen po'i rgyud:* Name of Dzogchen Tantra belonging to the Space Section.

lowest capacity will be confirmed in going to a natural nirmanakaya realm and will attain enlightenment without further bardo.

This chiefly depends upon one's present practice.

In this context, some people believe that teachings other than Dzogchen explain that one's consciousness will emerge [from the body] and the bardo of becoming will manifest if one fails to recognize the luminosity of the first bardo. Other than that, nothing is explained about the manifestations of sounds, colors, and lights or about the peaceful and wrathful deities. Those people think that if such things do manifest, they are a manifestation only of the particular deities of the practice one has done according to one's own dharma tradition and that it is impossible for everyone to experience the peaceful and wrathful deities of the Nyingma tradition.

Generally, there are indeed complete instructions on the bardos, in accordance with the particular stages of the path and oral instructions of each of the dharma traditions. Yet each individual tantra root text offers many differences in the emphasis of practice. Some give priority to the development stage. Some emphasize the practice of bliss and emptiness of the Path of Means. Others teach only to focus on simplicity. Numerous systems indeed exist. One's basis should be one's ability to apply in the bardo the particular practice with which one has presently been acquainted.

Through the Dzogchen Nyingthig system one can practice the teaching of Trekchö and Thögal as a unity. Having grown accustomed to such practice, the bardo will also manifest in that way. Then, by applying the practice, the basis is laid for attaining liberation.

Since the Thögal practice is not taught directly, other teachings also do not teach that such things will manifest in the bardo. However, because of the indivisible prana-mind composed of the five essences, the sounds, colors, and lights will always manifest. Texts such as the *Great Liberation from the Dangerous Pathway* underline that one is never separate from the ultimate nadi, prana and bindu. Moreover, the Kalachakra and Jordruk are similar to the system of the light and darkness practice of Dzogchen. Also, all the tantras agree that the deities perceived are the skandhas, elements, faculties, and sense bases of the beings who are, since the beginning, spontaneously perfect as the mandala itself.

Since, primordially, the five skandhas are the five buddha aspects, the five elements are the five consorts, the eight collections are the eight bodhisattvas, and the eight objects are the eight female bodhisattvas, and so forth, there are no deities which are not included within the so-called hundred sacred aspects. However, all the various body colors and attributes are explained only in terms of the different purifications of purification-basis and that which purifies. Besides that, there is actually not a single deity or mandala which is not included within the indivisible three kayas of self-cognizance or the unity of the two kayas.

Due to the power of one's individual tendencies and habits, it is not certain that deities other than the hundred sacred aspects may not manifest. Although sinful people may perceive the workmen of the Lord of Death, these are in fact nothing more than their own karmic experiences. In reality, no matter what appears or how it appears, the crucial point is recognizing it to be nothing but personal experiences. This is also stated in the *Domjung*:

> When the practitioners pass away,
> The herukas and so forth, and the yoginis,
> Holding various flowers in their hands
> As well as various banners and flags,

With different kinds of music
Send forth the sounds, "Death is but a thought!"
Thus are the practitioners led to the celestial realm.

This seems similar to the bardo of dharmata in the Nyingma system.

Moreover, the person who has realized whatever appears to be the display of the guru and also to be the great equal taste inseparable from self-cognizance, will indeed never depart from the dharmata realm of great bliss either in this life, the bardo or the next life. Otherwise it will be exactly as said in the *Khachö Lutreng:*

Like the confusion in the dreams of one's sleep last night,
Later on it will be difficult to practice in the bardo.

Passing one's days and nights in confusion and tenaciously clinging to a solid reality now, while one's body, speech, and mind are together and one has some freedom, will disappoint one's hopes of being able to rest in meditation during the intense pain at the moment of death, or when fears and delusions are swirling like a tornado. I think therefore that one must prepare oneself for the great and permanent goal.

CONCLUDING VERSES

The ground, the nature of the sugata-essence,
The path, the natural way of self-existing dharmakaya,
And the fruition, buddhahood realized free from
    defilements,
Are in reality one, indivisible in the present awareness.
Though this be so, like a treasure in the house of a poor
    man,
From beginningless time until now it has not been
    recognized.
Though recognized, without sustaining the natural state
It is spoiled and ruined by incessant confusion and
    clinging.

Maintain now undistractedly the mind-essence of
  whatever arises
In the awareness of the natural face as it is,
Without being fettered by the rigidity of mind-made
  meditation.
That will cut directly through all the bardos.

4
The Karmic Bardo
of Becoming

THE EXPLANATION of the nature of the karmic bardo of becoming is also in three parts.

IDENTIFYING THE ESSENCE

Dzogchen practitioners of higher and medium capacity will have been liberated in the earlier bardos. Practitioners of lesser capacity who have been unable to attain liberation, despite having seen the door of recognition during their lifetime, will next experience the dreamlike visions of the bardo of becoming. As a result, through the power of remembering former instructions and through the blessings of the truth of reality, they will be miraculously born from a lotus flower in a natural nirmanakaya realm, and, as when awakening from a dream, they will achieve the samadhi of awareness.

To the east, they will see the vision of Akshobhya and the emanations of the vajra family in the realm of True Joy. To the south, in the Splendorous Realm, they will be empowered by the emanations of the ratna family. To the west, in the realm of Lotus Mound, they will receive the prophecy[1] from the emanations of Amitabha. To the north, in the realm of Fulfilled Action, the emanations of the karma family will purify their habitual tendencies. And in the center, in the realm of Fully Liberating Sam-

---

1. The prediction of their future name as a fully and completely enlightened buddha.

sara, they will exhaust their obscurations of conceptual knowledge down to the most subtle aspects in the mandala of Glorious Heruka, the embodiment of the wrathful ones. Within five hundred years they will attain buddhahood in the great primordial purity of dharmakaya and act for the welfare of beings through innumerable emanations.

Some people in just one of the realms of the four directions receive empowerment, prophecy, and confirmation and then attain buddhahood. In short, such people experience the bardo of becoming only for a short while. They don't undergo all its sufferings and, without entering a womb, they reach a pure realm. This stage is therefore not considered the actual bardo of becoming. Thus the *Tantra of the Union of Sun and Moon* states:

> For the person of lower faculties who sees this [display],
> The intermediate state will change,
> Or it might also disappear.
> The teacher has said that these manifestations
> Bring an end to the tendency of habitual fixation.
> Being confirmed in going to a natural nirmanakaya realm,
> Buddhahood is attained without a bardo.

What, then, is the actual bardo of becoming? After body and mind have separated, the sounds, colors, and lights and so forth of the luminosity of dharmata disappear, due to their nature not having been recognized. The period from the arising of the confused tendencies up until one enters the womb of the next life is called the karmic bardo of becoming.

DETAILED EXPLANATION OF HOW ITS MANIFESTATIONS OCCUR

Ordinary persons do not possess the key points of oral instructions. In addition, their predominant karmic obscuration makes it difficult to form the right frame of mind or to arrange an auspicious coincidence through an instruction such as phowa. Even if they do perform phowa, it is extremely difficult for them to be able to transfer consciousness to the aimed object when they lack confidence and familiarity. They will therefore first experience the torments of the dissolution states.

When later the ground luminosity appears, most ordinary persons will lose consciousness. That is, not recognizing their nature, they become somewhat unconscious and, when the white and red essences finally emerge from the upper and lower openings, the consciousness will be blown away by the wind of karma, and will emerge through one of the nine openings.

At this time, one will be terrified by the natural sound of dharmata. One will be afraid of the manifestations of luminosity and want to flee from the light rays of compassion. One will panic from seeing the self-existing wisdom deities, as if they were the Lord of Death's workmen.

Although one perceives the scenery of the precious realms of spontaneous presence, all the phenomena of samsara and nirvana, as vividly as a reflection in a mirror, one dare not look towards the pure realms of the three kayas above. Instead, because of the solidifying power of one's former tendencies of clinging and unwholesome habits, one's mind becomes involved in the samsaric manifestations of the six realms below.

The luminosities of the innate nature are manifested due to the vital point of the former eighty inherent thought states and the winds of the elements having dissolved into the ground. But because of not recognizing their nature, now again, from the encompassing wind of ignorance, the wind-prana reappears and from that comes the wind of fire, from that the wind of water, and from that appears the wind of earth. Thus, the formation of smasara and the consciousness becoming more and more manifest and the seven thought states resulting from stupidity arise. From that again the confused thinking becomes more and more gross and so arise the forty thought states of desire and the thirty-three thought states of anger. By the power of the winds of the five elements combined with the consciousness, a mental body will manifest in a form that possesses all the sense faculties intact. One's body then has a slight radiance, it lives off scents, and one has the minor superknowledge of perceiving the minds of others.

One is able to travel, by a mere thought, to any place throughout the three-thousandfold world-system, except for the womb of one's future mother and Vajrasana.[2] One can be seen by people who have superknowledge, and by the bardo beings who are of the same type as oneself, but not by others.

One has suddenly assumed a form such that although one sees one's dead body, one still doesn't acknowledge having passed away. With strong attachment to one's house, wealth, and belongings, one will try to take possession of them. Seeing one's friends and family members use one's things, one will feel deprived and angry, much more than ever before, but they will not notice it.

Lacking the inner essences, the white and red elements, wherever one goes there is no outer light of the sun and the moon. Though tormented by hunger and thirst, one has no power to enjoy any food or drink that hasn't been especially dedicated to oneself. Lacking an actual material body, one roams about, here and there, to and fro, like a

---

2. According to some explanations, *Vajrasana* is taken literally to mean the Vajra Seat, the holy place in Bodh Gaya where Buddha Shakyamuni attained enlightenment. The great master Jigme Lingpa, however, holds that in this context it refers to the state of enlightenment itself.

feather blown in the wind, and experiences a feeling of pain much stronger than ever.

Furthermore, at this time there occur the six unfixed signs: (1) Without a fixed abode, one can transmigrate in an instant, and one seems to dwell without certainty in empty houses, tree stumps, crevices, or caves and so forth. (2) Without fixed support, one takes as refuge from pain the support of resting places such as various places of worship. (3) Without fixed behavior, one engages in various things every moment. (4) Without fixed food, one perceives the various good and bad foods of the six realms but cannot obtain them unless they are specially dedicated to oneself. (5) Without fixed companionship, one meets and keeps company for a short moment with the various gods, demons, ghosts, and beings of the bardo state. (6) Without fixed experiences, various kinds of mental perceptions, joys, and sorrows change every moment. One incessantly experiences innumerable terrors and hallucinations.

Moreover, the so-called four fearsome enemies appear: (1) Due to the earth-prana returning, one's personal experience is of being caught under a crumbling mountain or a collapsing house. (2) Due to the water-prana returning, one will feel as though being carried away by a huge river or sinking down into a great lake. (3) Due to the fire-prana returning, one will experience being burned within a blazing forest or house. (4) Due to the wind-prana returning, one will feel as if one is being blown away by a violent storm.

There are also the sufferings of falling into what appears as a terrifying, huge, white, red, and black abyss created by the natural forms of the tendencies of the three poisonous emotions. To this add being tormented by freezing rain storms, being caught under hail storms of pus and blood, or being chased by innumerable terrifying flesh-eating demons and carnivorous animals.

As a result of their severe evil actions of this life, fishermen, hunters, and butchers frequently have the deluded experience of being struck, beaten, killed, and cut up by many of the same kinds of animals they killed themselves in this lifetime.

In short, one will experience the miseries of the bardo of becoming for one to seven weeks or, for some, even for months and years. Generally, people remain for as long as seven weeks, once every week experiencing the pain of death. In brief, half of one's stay in the bardo is dominated by experiences of the habitual patterns of the present body and lifetime, and the remaining half consists mostly of the experiences of the following life.

About halfway through, one will experience arriving in the pale land of the dead in the presence of the Dharma-vajra Lord of the Dead, who is surrounded by a retinue of many terrible attendants. After this, one's innate god and demon separate one's acts of virtue and evil by dividing up white and black pebbles.

Beginning from this halfway point, one will experience one of the five light-paths of namjang, the natural manifestation of the coincidence of the karmic wind and the habitual patterns of the five poisons, which appear as a prediction of one's birthplace among the six classes of beings. If one is to be born as a god, the pale white light-path will appear. Similarly, for demigods, red appears, for humans blue, for animals green, and for hungry ghosts pale yellow. If one had the karma to be born in the hells, it is said that one would not have remained in this place but would have descended straightaway. Some texts teach that one will be born in the hells if one takes hold of the smoke-colored light.

The *Liberation through Hearing* states that these light-paths appear together with the lights of the combined four wisdoms mentioned above at the time that the deities of the five families manifest. This must be intended for certain types of individuals. For those who have been unable to take the five poisonous kleshas onto the path and have not realized them, the light-paths and birth places of six classes of being will now appear. However, practitioners who have realized these lights as having the nature of the five wisdoms will see them as the five wisdom lights and the five families of buddhas and will then be liberated into their essence.

At this point, according to the *Liberation through Hearing* and other texts, on the first day Buddha Akshobhya and his retinue will appear, on the second day Ratnasambhava, and so on. This teaching implies a sequence of a number of days. Few people however consider these to be actual solar days. Since they are, as described above, only meditation-days, understand that for ordinary people they do not appear for more than a short moment.

When, as a continuation of the above, one takes hold of any one of the five types of namjang, one understands that one has died and, emerging in the mental body of the bardo, one will despair and yearn to find a birthplace. By the power of that understanding, one will have the experience corresponding to one's specific karma for rebirth as one of the six classes of beings. One who is to be reborn as a god will have the vision of entering a celestial palace. One who is to be reborn as a demigod will experience entering a wheel of light. Some experience going into the middle of a battlefield. If one finds oneself in a cave, an earthen pit, or a straw nest, and so forth, one will be born as an animal. One who has a vision of a tree stump, a deep forest, or woven cloth becomes a hungry ghost. One who is born in the hells will feel that he is powerlessly being led down into a black pit or that he arrives in an iron city. There are also some who, being called by songs, entertainment, and lovers, cling to those visions and then find themselves reborn in the hells.

Individuals being reborn as humans have various kinds of visions. Seeing a lake adorned with male and female swans, one will be born at the eastern continent of the Superior Body; seeing a lake where female and male horses run about, one will be born on the northern continent of Unpleasant Sound; or seeing a lake adorned with cows, one will be born on the western continent of Cow Enjoyment. On this continent of Jambudvipa, one will either be born as an ordinary human in one of the unfree states if one feels that one is entering into a mist, or one will attain a precious human body if one has the experience of arriving in a mansion or city or among many people.

Seeing one's father and mother engaged in intercourse, one will feel jealousy or desire towards either the father or the mother, depending on whether one is to be born as a male or a female. That causes one to connect with them and thus enter into the womb.

Those beings who are miraculously born—born from heat and moisture and so forth—will enter that place of birth due to a thought of either attachment or anger.

CONCLUDING EXPLANATION OF HOW TO APPLY THE INSTRUCTIONS

From this very day one must by all means interrupt the wheel of the twelve links of interdependence of the fearsome and terrifying sufferings, which spin again and again uninterruptedly like the rim of a water wheel. Therefore familiarize yourself from now on with the key points of instruction as repeatedly explained above. The best advice, which alone will suffice, is to remain inseparable from wakefulness, the practice of gaining mastery over one own's mind. Orgyen Rinpoche himself has said:

One may wonder why it is that one can attain stability merely by recognizing one's nature for one instant at the time of the bardo. The reply is that at present the mind is encased in the net of the wind of karma, the wind of karma is encased in the net of the material body of flesh and blood, and therefore one has no independence. After this body has separated into matter and mind, the prana-mind, along with its magical displays, has no concrete material support during the period in which one has not yet become encased in the net of the future body. One has independence while the mind lacks a material basis, and can therefore recognize one's nature. One's capacity to attain stability by merely recognizing is like a torch which in one instant can clear away the darkness of aeons. If one has recognition in the bardo just as one now has when receiving the pointing-out instruction, then there is no doubt about attaining enlightenment. Therefore, from this very moment, make yourself acquainted.

Aspiration, in particular, is of the utmost importance as the essential point of all the dream and bardo trainings. This means that one should be continuously mindful and determined, thinking: "What I do now is like dream and illusion! I have died and arrived in the bardo! All my experiences are bardo experiences! I should apply the specific key points of practice!" With such determination, one cannot avoid being adept in the bardo.

Most ordinary people, however, are solidly fixated, thinking: "These present experiences are completely real! They are actual! I am not dead!" That type of action indeed leaves no chance whatsoever for recognition in the bardo. Moreover, it is never taught that people who cling to this life will have any success in dharma practice. Therefore, exert yourself as Milarepa said:

> Dying being my only fear,
> I trained my mind in the innate state beyond death,
> And recognized the essential meaning,
> The basic nature of self-liberated samsara.
>
> This unsupported and naked inner awareness,
> Discursiveness cleared, the confidence of the view,
> I have resolved to be empty luminosity.
> Birth and death no longer intimidate me.

As long as one has not taken hold of the luminosity of namjang, one must in all situations resolve that the terrifying experiences that take place, no matter of what type, are the self-display of one's own mind. In particular, matchless Gampopa's advice on *Bringing the Four Enemies into the Path* and other such instructions are clearly of utmost importance.

If one has gained some degree of mastery in the instructions on dreaming and has at present become skilled in conjuring emanations, developing skill, and especially in cultivating pure lands, one will be able to achieve whatever one wishes simply by remembering the key points. In the context of Dzogchen, in accord with what was explained above, to gain mastery over the pure realm of personal experience, one will train in the special paths and levels in those pure realms of natural nirmanakaya and thus without difficulty quickly realize the great enlightenment. The training in the phowa of the celestial realm is also similar to this [practice for the bardo of becoming].

In any case, one must avoid becoming engaged, owing to power of present tendencies and bad habits, in feeling attached to one's material things, friends, and attendants and so forth or in entertaining thoughts of like or dislike toward whatever one sees as unfinished works left behind or toward good or bad groups of people. Many stories in the sutras and elsewhere exemplify why this is important. So, without clinging to anything whatsoever, one should exert oneself one-pointedly in the practice.

Once one has taken hold of one of the namjang luminosities, turning back is quite difficult. Yet, regardless of what one perceives at that time, such as a link for rebirth in the form of the father and the mother of the next lifetime, one should at best rest evenly in the blissful and empty state of coemergent wisdom according to Mahamudra, or in the state of awareness and emptiness according to Dzogchen. That is the supreme method for blocking the gate of the womb, called stopping the enterer.

If one lacks such capacity but has attained confidence in the correct development stage and is thus able to emerge in a pure illusory body or in a wisdom form, uniting appearance and emptiness, one will attain the sambhogakaya in the bardo. The Sarma and Nyingma schools all teach this. For such attainment one needs to be already adept in such meditation through correct understanding of the symbol, meaning, and sign of the development stage. But nowadays, due to the times, most people who consider themselves development stage practitioners meditate with strong clinging to their solidified or conceptualized development stage. Such meditations are only done with the attitude of hoping to pacify sicknesses or negative influences of this lifetime or to gain some power to accomplish one of the minor common activities. Otherwise, people who engage in a flawless practice of deity and mantra for the sake of complete enlightenment seem extremely rare. So, forget about such a development stage of solid fixation being the cause of liberation in the bardo; just consider how one can be born as a hungry ghost in the form of one's yidam.

If one understands the development stage correctly, one should imagine whomever one sees—the objects of desire, anger, or jealousy, such as one's father and mother—to be the yidam with consort. That will also be a supreme cause for blocking the gate of rebirth.

If one intentionally wants to take rebirth in a human body so that one can practice the dharma, one should visualize oneself and one's parents as deities and enter the womb while possessing the samadhis such as the five aspects of true enlightenment or the three rituals. Doing that, one will achieve whatever one desires.

If one is a monastic practitioner who cherishes the precious trainings, one should, when seeing the father and mother who are the link to a rebirth, cast far away the feelings, thoughts, and deeds of either lust or aggression by means of one-pointed determination in one's discipline. Firm revulsion and renunciation can also close the door to the evil states of samsara. Therefore, at this very moment train yourself in the frame of mind acquainted with such renunciation.

Furthermore, without experience in any of these practices, one will be chased about by the terrors of the bardo, forcefully leading one to evil states of rebirth. When that happens, call upon the master and the three jewels for rescue and take refuge in them. If one can supplicate them one-pointedly, one will be liberated from the terrors by the power of their unfailing compassion, and, taking rebirth in a body endowed with the freedoms and riches in which one can practice the dharma, one will before long attain enlightenment. These last means are called blocking the birth gate to the place of entering.

If one cannot block the birth gate in those ways, methods for choosing the place of birth are taught. In short, all the important points of instruction for the bardos are included within the above.

Moreover, when an ordinary person is on the verge of dying, he should be placed with his right side on the mat. One can recite blessed scriptures at the top of his head such as the names of the buddhas, dharani mantras, and so forth. According to some instructions one can perform the substance phowa and also use the blessed samaya substance and so forth. In short, do whatever possible to arrange for the various kinds of auspicious coincidences which save beings from the lower realms.

After someone's death, one should perform the pure mandala rituals of vajrayana, have the words of the sugatas read aloud, make purification rituals, confer empowerments, or burn the name inscription and so forth. If these steps are done, then through the truth of the unfailing interdependence of cause and effect, through the compassion of the victorious ones, and through the truth of the nature of things, immense benefit will result.

Based on that, however, regardless of whether the performers of these rituals have a correct samadhi, if they behave improperly or have a perverted attitude or conduct, then, since the deceased person can see that with his supersensory perceptions, a danger exists that he will thereby connect with an unfortunate rebirth. A pure attitude is therefore essential.

In particular, using virtuous offerings and donations for the sake of the dead as an excuse for slaughter of animals will, instead of helping, cause even greater harm. Since all the sutras and tantras state this, it is indeed of vital importance not to mingle with wrongdoing any virtuous deed of any size being done after the death.

For those who have entered the gate of the profound practices it shouldn't matter whether virtuous deeds are performed after their death. If one does not already make it unnecessary to hope for such things, one's dharma practice is superfluous. As Orgyen has said:

> Exert yourself in the sacred dharma before passing away.
> When empowerment is conferred on your name
> inscription[3] it will be too late.
> As your mind roams through the bardo like a starved
> dog,
> Thinking of the higher realms will be difficult.

Shang Rinpoche has said:

> Donning armor after being wounded,
> Regretting misdeeds on the verge of death,
> And empowering the corpse after its dying
> Are of course all right, but is it not too late?

Therefore endeavor to practice while in this body. If you can practice, condensing all the points into one, then there is no obstruction for the means of dharma. Phadampa has said:

> One is not ruined from not knowing the dharma.
> One is ruined from being unable to practice.
> How can there be one who doesn't know the six syllables?
> But there are indeed some who don't recite them.

Therefore, exert yourself with certainty. As Dampa Künga said:

> If you have certainty, you never lack the instructions.
> Seek not the hearing lineage elsewhere, you people of Dingri.

Thus, concentrate on practicing whatever you incline towards or are familiar with, and then make yourself, for best results, delighted to die; second best, without fear; or

---

3. A ritual purification performed for ordinary people after their death, during which the name on a piece of paper is used.

at least free from regret. This is the instruction of the most essential point.

CONCLUDING VERSES

Kyema!
From beginningless time until now
I have been always sinking in the ocean of samsara, but
   still I don't feel weary.
Precious Ones, please turn to virtue this mind of mine,
The dharma-pretender who strives for the aims of this
   life.

With no thought for life and limb when pursuing
   nondharmic things,
But unable to bear a single hardship for dharma's sake.
With perverted perseverance, like a madman jumping in
   the river—
Please heed us, the dharma-charlatans who fill the land.

Boasting of being learned while giving the doctrine a bad
   name,
Pretending to be virtuous while filled with nonvirtue—
This predominant custom, like excrement enveloped in
   silk,
Is the light of the setting sun of the Buddha's teachings.

With the freedoms and riches like mountain mist of the
   verge of dissolving,
And one's life span fast running away like a mountain
   stream,
Yet without leisure, preparing as though to remain for
   one hundred years,
Now the time is surely right to quickly prepare for death.

Preparations and aims out of fear of not being counted
   among people,
Hoarding wealth out of fear of starving in one's old age,
And the studious effort of desiring a vast knowledge of
   words—
There is now no time for doing any of these things.

Kyeho!
Recognize these manifold appearances, as a dream,

To be your personal experiences, illusory and unreal.
Without fixating on anything, maintain self-cognizance
beyond concepts.
That is the essential practice of the bardo of this life.

You will certainly die soon, and then nothing will be of
real help.
The death experience is only your own conceptual
thinking.
Without constructing thoughts, abandon them in the
space of self-cognizance.
That is the essential practice of the bardo of dying.

The fixation on appearance or disappearance, as being
good or bad, is your mind.
This mind is the self-expression of dharmakaya perceiving
whatever there is.
Not to cling, make concepts, accept, or reject what is
perceived,
That is the essential practice of the bardo of dharmata.

Samsara is your mind and nirvana is also your mind.
Pleasure, pain, and deluded experiences exist nowhere
apart from your mind.
To attain mastery over your own mind,
That is the essential practice of the bardo of becoming.

Since your self-cognizance is never separated from the
three kayas,
It is utterly devoid of attributes of this life, the next, and
the bardo.
Yet the confusion of the bardo appears for the mind that
has not realized this.
It is essential to take exactly what appears as the path.

The various personal experiences appearing to yourself
Are not cast away by discarding, nor can they be stopped
by blocking them off.
Yet, recognizing their nature, you are freed from the
causes and conditions for confusion.
All the key points are condensed into just this.

Follow therefore carefully a sacred master
And resolve your doubts about the concise essence of all
the teachings.

With the discipline of equalizing your life span with your
   practice,
Exert yourself in quickly accomplishing the welfare of
   yourself and others.

"Since all the key points of the essential practices of the
   secret mantra of true meaning
Can be condensed into these four bardo states,
Please explain their divisions and ways of condensing
   them."
Having been urged in that way by one called Aspiration,[4]
   I have therefore uttered this.

Someone like me who has not studied or reflected upon
   the scriptural traditions
And possesses not even a fraction of meditation
   experience,
Will not have power to delight or benefit others through
   uttering this,
But only to exhaust himself with words.

When nowadays the books of the Buddha's words and the
   root texts of the learned and accomplished ones
Are mostly made into nests for insects and worms,
How can any intelligent person take delight
In this, my composition of ordinary words?

However, in order not to go against
The words of him who requested this,
I have here, as best I could,
Written down what I have heard from some kind teachers'
   voices.

By whatever noble virtue there may be from confessing all
   faults and mistakes,
May all my old mothers in endless samsara attain
   complete enlightenment,
And may all directions and times be filled with the
   auspicious goodness
Of the Buddha's immaculate teachings, forever shining as
   a torch for those to be tamed.

---

4. The name of the person who requested these teachings.

Epilogue

TOGETHER with a ganachakra, Kalden Mönlam (Worthy Aspiration) made this request: "We need a detailed and lucid composition on the manifestation of the bardos, the defects and virtues, and how one should practice, which accords with the general meaning of all the New and Old Schools of the Secret Mantra." But because my eyesight of learning and contemplation is weak and even the little I have learned falls under the power of forgetfulness, I cannot express anything definitely. However, I have written down here all I could from whatever I have read in a few scriptures and on top of that added some fragments of whatever I have heard from a few kind teachers.

If what is written here has many faults, such as incorrectness, contradictions, or repetitions due to my undiscerning ignorance, I beg not to be despised by intelligent, learned, and accomplished people.

This was written by Natsok Rangdröl while in retreat at the forest hermitage of Glorious Götsangpa. May it be virtuous.

Translator's Afterword

According to clarifications by Tulku Urgyen Rinpoche and Chökyi Nyima Rinpoche, this was translated by Erik Pema Kunsang at Ka-Nying Shedrup Ling and Nagi Gompa, 1986.

VERSES OF DEDICATION

Although the ground space is utterly pure from the
 beginning,
Beings wander through the bardo states due to not
 recognizing the nature of the ground-manifestations.
By the virtue of publishing this gift of dharma—
The General Points of the Bardo,
The profound and secret words of Natsok Rangdröl, who
 reached perfection in the four visions
And compassionately liberates all beings from the ocean
 of samsara—
May the teachings of the Buddha flourish,
And may the entire three realms attain the result of the
 four kayas.[1]

---

1. These verses, by an unknown author, were found at the end of our Tibetan manuscript.

APPENDIX

The Dzogchen Tantras

THE FOLLOWING INFORMATION is a summary of the teachings of Vimalamitra, Longchenpa, and Khenpo Ngakchung as recorded in the Nyingthig Yabshi and its related commentaries.

The first human vidyadhara in the Dzogchen lineage was Garab Dorje, who compiled the 6,400,000 tantras of the Great Perfection. He entrusted these teachings to his main disciple, Manjushrimitra, who then classified them into the Three Sections of Dzogchen: Mind Section, Space Section, and Instruction Section.

The chief disciple of Manjushrimitra, the great master known as Shri Singha, divided the Instruction Section into The Four Cycles of Nyingthig: the Outer, Inner, Secret, and Innermost Unexcelled Cycles.

The Innermost Unexcelled Cycle consists of seventeen tantras. There are eighteen when adding the *Ngagsung Trömay Tantra,* which is focused on the protective rites of Ekajati. According to the system of Padmakara, there are nineteen when including the *Longsel Barwey Tantra.*

These tantras teach in full all the requirements for one person to practice and attain complete buddhahood within a single lifetime. Each tantra is not dependent upon the others but is complete in itself.

Appendix

1. *Dra Thalgyur Root Tantra* (sgra thal 'gyur rtsa ba'i rgyud) explains how to attain the level of nirmanakaya and how to accomplish the welfare of others through practices related to sound.

2. *The Tantra of Graceful Auspiciousness* (bkra shis mdzes ldan gyi rgyud) teaches how to establish the nature of awareness and how to identify the basis of confusion and the unmistaken wisdom.

3. *The Tantra of the Heart Mirror of Samantabhadra* (kun tu bzang po thugs kyi me long) shows how to identify and cut through pitfalls and errors and how to establish what is innate.

4. *The Blazing Lamp Tantra* (sgron ma 'bar ba'i rgyud) teaches how to identify the "lamps" related to awareness, their terminology, analogies for how wisdom arises, the unity of awareness, how to clear misconceptions about self-cognizance, and how to practice.

5. *The Tantra of the Mind Mirror of Vajrasattva* (rdo rje sems dpa' snying gi me long) teaches how the lamps are the self-display of awareness. By means of twenty-one pointing-out instructions, the different types of people recognize wisdom. It further teaches the four key points and how to practice.

6. *The Tantra of Self-Manifest Awareness* (rig pa rang shar gyi rgyud) teaches how to resolve the view, meditation, and action.

7. *The Tantra of Studded Jewels* (nor by bkra bkod) shows how to eliminate the defects and sidetracks connected to the view and the practice of meditation, conduct, and fruition.

8. *The Tantra of Pointing-Out Instructions* (ngo sprod sprad pa'i rgyud) describes applying the essence of awareness in one's practice through various indications.

9. *The Tantra of the Six Spheres of Samantabhadra* (kun tu bzang po klong drug pa'i rgyud) teaches how to purify and prevent rebirth in the six realms and manifest the pure realms of self-display.

10. *The Tantra of No Letters* (yi ge med pa'i rgyud) describes the actual means of practice, how to abandon activities and live in places free from defects, the four ways of "freely resting," sustaining naturalness, and the undefiled method of the main part of practice.

11. *The Tantra of the Perfected Lion* (seng ge rtsal rdzogs kyi rgyud) explains the degrees of progress and the signs that occur, how to stabilize awareness, and how to increase the level of experience.

12. *The Pearl Garland Tantra* (mu tig phreng ba'i rgyud) is taught for the sake of preventing awareness from straying back by means of bringing it to maturation. It teaches how to practice and how to reach familiarity and liberation.

13. *The Tantra of Self-Liberated Awareness* (rig pa rang grol gyi rgyud) teaches how awareness is uncreated but is liberated by itself, how to control appearances, how to grow familiar with the vajra chain, and how to naturally free all from samsara and nirvana.

14. *The Tantra of Piled Gems* (rin chen spungs pa'i

rgyud) explains how all the manifest qualities
are all the essence of space and awareness.

15. *The Tantra of Shining Relics* (sku gdung 'bar
ba'i rgyud) describes the outer and inner signs
of awareness reaching maturity which are
manifest before and after the time of death in
order to inspire and instill confidence in other
persons.

16. *The Union of Sun and Moon Tantra* (nyi zla kha
sbyor) shows which experience a person undergoes in the intermediate state (bardo) after
passing away. It teaches how to resolve one's
master's oral instructions during the bardo of
this life, how to stabilize awareness during the
bardo of dying, how to attain enlightenment
through recognizing awareness during the
bardo of dharmata, and, if necessary, how to
be assured a rebirth in a natural nirmanakaya
realm during the bardo of becoming and there
attain buddhahood without further rebirths.

17. *The Tantra of Self-Existing Perfection* (rdzogs pa
rang byung) teaches how to prepare to be a
suitable recipient of the teachings by means of
the four empowerments.

18. *The Tantra of the Black Wrathful Shri Ekajati*
(dpal e ka dza ti nag mo khros ma'i rgyud)
describes how to protect the practitioner
against harms inflicted by others.

Vimalamitra united the explanatory lineage with scriptures and the hearing lineage without scriptures and concealed them, to be revealed in the future as the Nyingthig
teachings renowned as Vima Nyingthig, and also as the
Secret Heart Essence of Vimalamitra (bi ma'i gsang ba

snying thig). Longchenpa clarified them in his fifty-one sections of Lama Yangthig.

Padmakara concealed his teachings on the Innermost Unexcelled Cycle, to be revealed in the future as Khandro Nyingthig, the Heart Essence of the Dakinis. Longchenpa also clarified these teachings in his Khandro Yangthig.

These four exceptional sets of Dzogchen instructions are contained, together with Longchenpa's additional teachings Zabmo Yangthig, in his collection famed as Nyingthig Yabshi.

In recent years, many Westerners have had the fortune to receive this collection in completeness from living masters headed by His Holiness Dilgo Khyentse Rinpoche, Pema Norbu Rinpoche, and Dodrup Chen Rinpoche, and in parts by the masters who have passed on the transmissions for Jamgon Kongtrul's precious treasuries, the Rinchen Terdzo and Damngak Dzo.

GLOSSARY

THIS GLOSSARY was compiled partly from questions to Tulku Chökyi Nyima Rinpoche and Tulku Urgyen Rinpoche, to give general readers a rough idea about the different uncommon expressions used in the translation. The translator has tried to refrain from personal interpretations and kept strictly to what he has heard from his teachers. This glossary does not attempt to give exhaustive explanations. The Tibetan equivalents have been included so that one can have the more profound terms clarified by Tibetan-speaking masters. Many of the English terms were coined exclusively for use in this translation and may have been phrased differently in another context.

ACCOMPLISHMENTS (dngos grub, siddhi) *See* supreme and common siddhis.

ACCUMULATION OF MERIT (bsod nams kyi tshogs) Virtuous actions with concepts.

ACCUMULATION OF WISDOM (ye shes kyi tshogs) Virtuous actions embraced by the discriminating knowledge (shes rab) of insight into emptiness.

ACHARYA NAGARJUNA (slob dpon klu sgrub) A great Indian master of philosophy. He was named "Naga Master" because he taught the beings in the naga world and returned with the extensive version of Prajnaparamita left in their safekeeping.

ADI BUDDHA SAMANTABHADRA (mdod ma'i sangs rgyas kun tu bzang po) The primordially enlightened buddha.

AFFLICTED MIND CONSCIOUSNESS (nyon yid kyi rnam shes) A term used in the abhidharma teachings. One of the eight consciousnesses, it harbors the thought "I am" and is the basis for all negative emotions. Also one of the eight collections.

AKANISHTA REALM ('og min gyi zhing) The highest buddha realm.

AKSHOBYHA (mi bskyod pa) The chief buddha of the vajra family.

ALL-ACCOMPLISHING WISDOM (bya grub ye shes) One of the five wisdoms.

ALL-ENCOMPASSING PURITY (dag pa rab 'byams) All the components of our existence, the skandhas, elements, and so forth of the world and of all beings, are, in their pure aspects, a pure realm consisting of the five male and female buddhas and so forth; so, when perceiving things as they are, there is not even a speck of impurity to find anywhere. This is the basic view of the Anuttara Tantra of the New Schools and the Three Inner Tantras of the Old School. For more information see Longchen Rabjam's *phyogs bcu mun sel,* recently translated by Gyurme Dorje.

ALL-ENCOMPASSING PURITY OF APPEARANCE AND EXISTENCE (snang srid dag pa rab 'byams) A term used especially in the teachings of the maha, anu, and ati tantras, demonstrating that all phenomena are inherently perfect.

ALL-GROUND (kun gzhi, alaya) This word has different meanings in different contexts and should be understood accordingly. Literally it means the "foundation of all things."

ALL-PERVASIVE SUFFERING OF BEING CONDITIONED (khyab pa 'du byed kyi sdug bsngal) The third of the three sufferings. It consists in the continuation of the five aggregates that perpetuate conditioned existence in samsara.

AMITABHA (snang ba mtha' yas). One of the five buddhas; the chief figure of the lotus family.

ANU (rjes su [rnal 'byor]) The second of the three inner tantras: maha, anu, and ati. The emphasis of this tantra is the buddha-mandala contained within the vajra body of the yidam, and the chief practice is completion stage with concepts.

APERTURE OF BRAHMA (tshangs bug) The opening at the top of one's head, eight fingers above the hairline.

Glossary

APPARENT LUMINOSITY (snang ba'i 'od gsal)   The luminosity of the manifest aspect. Compare with *empty luminosity*.

APPEARANCE AND EXISTENCE (snang srid)   Whatever can be experienced and has a possibility of existence. Usually this term refers to the world and sentient beings.

APPEARANCE, INCREASE, AND ATTAINMENT (snang mched thob gsum)   The three stages in the process of dissolution, either at the moment of dying or when falling asleep.

ATI (shin tu [rnal 'byor])   The third of the three inner tantras. Ati yoga is a synonym for Dzogchen (Skt. *mahasandhi*). The emphasis of this tantra is the buddha-mandala contained within the nature of mind, and the chief practices are the completion stages without concepts, known as trekchö and thögal.

ATTAINMENT (thob pa)   The third of the three experiences of appearance, increase, and attainment.

AVALOKITESHVARA (spyan ras gzigs)   (1) The embodiment of compassion. (2) One of the eight main bodhisattvas.

BARDO OF BECOMING (srid pa'i bar do)   The period after death from the arising of confusion and one's emergence in a mental body until being conceived in the womb of the next life.

BARDO OF DHARMATA (chos nyid kyi bar do)   The period from dying until emerging in the mental body of the bardo of becoming.

BARDO OF DYING ('chi kha'i bar do)   The period from catching a fatal sickness until the end of the three dissolution stages.

BARDO OF THIS LIFE (skye gnas kyi bar do)   The period from conception in the womb until catching a fatal disease or meeting with an irreversible cause of death.

BARDO STATE (bar do'i srid pa).   Usually this term refers to the intermediate state between death and the next rebirth, but in this context it means "gap" or "period" between two things. Sometimes it is translated as "intermediate state."

BHUMIS (sa)   The ten bodhisattva levels.

BINDUS   (1) The red and white essences. (2) Spheres or circles.

BLACKNESS (nag lam) An experience of utter blackness, the third stage of appearance, increase, and attainment.

BLISSFUL REALM (bde ba can, Sukhavati) The pure land of Buddha Amitabha.

BODHICITTA (byang sems, byang chub kyi sems) (1) The aspiration to attain enlightenment for the sake of all beings. (2) The red and white essences.

BODHICITTA OF APPLICATION ('jug pa'i byang chub kyi sems) This is composed chiefly of the six paramitas.

BODHICITTA OF ASPIRATION (smon pa'i byang chub kyi sems) This is composed chiefly of the four immeasurables: compassion, love, sympathetic joy, and impartiality.

BODHISATTVA (byang chub sems dpa') Someone who has developed bodhicitta, the aspiration to attain enlightenment in order to benefit all sentient beings.

BODHISATTVA TRAININGS (byang chub sems dpa'i bslab pa) The precepts and practices of a bodhisattva.

BODY OF LIGHT ('od kyi lus) The body of light of the five wisdoms, devoid of materiality.

BÖN (bon) The religion in Tibet before Buddhism. When used with a negative connotation, it means the use of rituals for mundane or selfish pursuits.

BUDDHA SHAKYAMUNI (sangs rgyas sha kya thub pa) The historical Buddha.

CAUSAL VEHICLES (rgyu'i theg pa) Hinayana and mahayana. The emphasis of these teachings is to regard the path as the cause for attaining fruition: liberation from samsara or complete buddhahood. The resultant vehicles of vajrayana, on the other hand, regard the fruition of buddhahood as being inherently present within all beings, and the path is simply the act of removing the temporary obscurations that prevent us from receiving this correctly.

CHANNELS, WINDS, AND ESSENCES (rtsa rlung thig le) Nadi, prana, and bindu; the constituents of the vajra body.

CHETSUN SENGE WANGCHUK. A great master of the Nyingma Lineage. *Chetsun* means "Noble-Tongued," someone who never lied, slandered, or gossiped. At the verge of passing away in the rainbow body of five-colored light, at Oyuk Lung in Central Tibet, he imparted his last instructions, the epitome of the Dzogchen teachings, to the dakini Palgyi Lodrö. Many centuries later, the great nonsectarian master Jamyang Khyentse Wangpo had a visionary experience recalling his former incarnation as Chetsun Senge Wangchuk and was given the teachings back by the dakini. He wrote them down as the *Chetsun Nyingthig,* the Heart Essence of Chetsun, a cycle of teachings that is one of the most important Dzogchen tantras to be practiced in the coming generations.

CHILD LUMINOSITY (bu'i 'od gsal)   The experience of luminosity in one's present meditation practice, while on the path. *See* mother luminosity.

CHÖD (gcod)   Pronounced *choe.* Literally, "cutting." A system of practices set down by Machik Labdrön for the purpose of cutting through the four Maras. One of the Eight Practice Lineages of Buddhism in Tibet.

CHÖDRUK (chos drug)   The Six Doctrines.

CHÖKYI NYIMA RINPOCHE (chos kyi nyi ma rin po che)   The abbot of Ka-Nying Shedrup Ling Monastery in the Kathmandu valley of Nepal and the oldest son of Tulku Urgyen Rinpoche.

CHÖYUL (gcod yul)   Synonymous with Chöd.

COEMERGENT IGNORANCE (lhan cig skyes pa'i ma rig pa)   *Coemergent* means arising together with or coexistent with one's mind, like sandalwood and its fragrance. *Ignorance* here means lack of knowledge of the nature of mind.

COEMERGENT WISDOM (lhan cig skyes pa'i ye shes)   The innate wakefulness potentially present in all sentient beings.

COMMON AND SUPREME SIDDHIS (thun mong dang mchog gi dngos grub)   Usually this term refers to the eight common siddhis and the supreme siddhi of mahamudra.

COMPLETION STAGE (rdzogs rim)   The completion stage with concepts is the Six Doctrines of Naropa according to the Sarma schools or Anu Yoga in the Nyingma system; the completion stage without concepts is Essence Mahamudra according to Sarma or Dzogchen in the Nyingma system.

Glossary

CONFUSED EXPERIENCES ('khrul snang) All the experiences of ordinary people which, like the dream state, are regarded as being real and solid.

CULMINATED AWARENESS (rig pa tshad phebs) The third of the four visions in Dzogchen.

CULTIVATING PURE REALMS (dag pa'i zhing sbyong ba) A practice connected with dream yoga.

CUTTING (gcod). Synonymous with *chöd*.

CYCLIC EXISTENCE ('khor ba, samsara) *Samsara* means to spin or circle endlessly, as on a potter's wheel or on the rim of a water wheel. The idea is that sentient beings take birth and die, endlessly, in the six realms of samsara: the abodes of hell-beings, hungry ghosts, animals, humans, demigods, and gods.

DAKA (dpa' bo) Male enlightened practitioner of vajrayana. Can also have deeper levels of meaning.

DAKINI (mkha' 'gro ma) One of the three roots. Spiritual beings who fulfill the enlightened activities.

DAMPA KUNGA (dam pa kun dga') The Indian master Phadampa Sangye, who brought the teachings of Shije to Tibet.

DEMIGOD (lha ma yin). One of the six classes of beings.

DEVELOPMENT AND COMPLETION (bskyed rdzogs) The two main aspects of vajrayana practice. By uniting the means (upaya) of the development stage, the fabricated, with the knowledge (prajña) of the completion stage, the unfabricated, a tantric practitioner swiftly attains complete enlightenment.

DEVELOPMENT MAHAYOGA (bskyed pa ma ha yo ga) The first of the three inner tantras; emphasizes the development stage.

DEVELOPMENT STAGE (bskyed rim, utpattikrama) One of the two aspects of vajrayana practice, which involves mentally creating pure images in order to purify habitual tendencies. *See* stages of development and completion.

DHARANI MANTRAS (gzungs sngags) Long mantras, used for various purposes.

DHARMA-DOOR (chos kyi sgo mo) A particular teaching whose practice is the entrance to the path of enlightenment.

DHARMA-MUDRA (chos kyi phyag rgya) One of the four mudras.

DHARMADHATU (chos kyi dbyings) The "realm of phenomena." Same as emptiness. In this context, *dharma* means the truth, and *dhatu* means space free from center or periphery. Another explanation is "the nature of phenomena," which is beyond arising, dwelling, and ceasing.

DHARMADHATU WISDOM (chos kyi dbyings kyi ye shes) One of the five wisdoms.

DHARMAKAYA (chos sku) The first of the three kayas.

DHARMAKAYA DISPLAY (chos sku'i snang ba).

DHARMAKAYA LUMINOSITY OF PRIMORDIAL PURITY (ka dag chos sku'i 'od gsal) The Dzogchen word for our enlightened essence in its naked state.

DHARMATA (chos nyid) The nature of phenomena.

DHARMATA EXHAUSTION BEYOND CONCEPTS (chos zad blo 'das) The fourth of the four visions in Dzogchen.

DISCRIMINATING WISDOM (so sor rtog pa'i ye shes) One of the five wisdoms.

DISSOLUTION STAGES (thim rim) A process of physical and mental dissolution that all sentient beings go through at various times, as when falling asleep and even in the moment of a sneeze. Here these stages refer chiefly to the process of dying.

DREAM (rmi lam) Here specifically referring to one of the Six Doctrines of Naropa.

DZOGCHEN (rdzogs pa chen po, rdzogs chen). The teachings beyond the vehicles of causation, first taught in the world of human beings by the great vidyadhara Garab Dorje.

DZOGCHEN NYINGTHIG The Heart Essence of the Great Perfection. Specifically the teachings of Dzogchen brought to Tibet by Vimalamitra and Guru Rinpoche and later set down by Longchenpa.

EARLY SPREAD OF THE TEACHINGS (bstan pa snga dar) *See* Early Translations.

EARLY TRANSLATIONS (sngar 'gyur) The teachings translated into Tibetan before the great translator Rinchen Sangpo, during the reigns of the Tibetan kings Trisong Deutsen and Ralpachen in the ninth and tenth centuries.

EIGHT BODHISATTVAS (byang chub sems dpa' brgyad) *See* Eight main bodhisattvas.

EIGHT COLLECTIONS (tshogs brgyad) The eight collections of consciousnesses/cognitions.

EIGHT COMMON SIDDHIS (thun mong gi dngos grub brgyad) Eight types of mundane miraculous powers.

EIGHT CONSCIOUSNESSES (rnam shes tshogs brgyad) The all-ground consciousness, mind-consciousness, afflicted mind-consciousness, and the five sense-consciousnesses.

EIGHT DOORS TO SAMSARA ('khor ba'i sgo brgyad) The eight openings of one's body, not counting the aperture at the top of one's head.

EIGHT FEMALE BODHISATTVAS (byang chub sems ma brgyad) Lasya, Mala, Gita, Nirti, Pushpa, Dhupa, Aloka, and Gandha.

EIGHT FREEDOMS (dal ba brgyad) Not being in the three lower realms, not being a long-living god, not having wrong views, not a savage, not a mute, and not born in an age without buddhas.

EIGHT MAIN BODHISATTVAS (nye ba'i sras brgyad) Kshitigarbha, Akashagarbha, Avalokiteshvara, Vajrapani, Maitreya, Sarvanirvarana-vishkambin, Samatabhadra, and Manjushri.

EIGHT OBJECTS (yul brgyad) The objects of the eight consciousnesses: sight, sound smell, taste, texture, mental objects, the all-ground, and appearance.

EIGHT PRACTICE LINEAGES (sgrub brgyud shing rta brgyad) The eight independent schools of Buddhism that flourished in Tibet: Nyingma, Kadampa, Marpa Kagyü, Shangpa Kagyü, Sakya, Jordruk, Shije, and Chöd.

EIGHT SIDDHIS (dngos grub brgyad) The eight types of mundane, or common, accomplishments.

EIGHT WORLDLY CONCERNS ('jig rten chos brgyad) Attachment to gain, pleasure, praise, and fame and aversion to loss, pain, bad reputation, and blame.

Glossary

EIGHTY INHERENT THOUGHT STATES (rang bzhin brgyad cu'i rtog pa) Thirty-three resulting from anger, forty from desire, and seven from delusion. (See list included in text.)

EMANCIPATION AND OMNISCIENCE (thar pa dang thams cad mkhyen pa) Liberation from samsara and perfect buddhahood.

EMPTY LUMINOSITY (stong pa'i 'od gsal) The unmanifest aspect of luminosity.

ETERNALISM (rtag lta) The extreme view that the individual self, objective phenomena, and a creator god exist as something independent, everlasting, and singular.

EXHAUSTION OF PHENOMENA BEYOND CONCEPTS (chos zad blo 'das) The fourth of the four visions of Dzogchen.

EXISTENCE AND PEACE (srid zhi) Synonymous with *samsara* and *nirvana*.

EXPERIENCE OF ATTAINMENT (thob pa'i nyams) The third of the three stages of appearance, increase, and attainment. Same as the "redness."

EXPERIENCE OF INCREASE (mched pa'i nyams) The second of the stages of appearance, increase, and attainment. Same as the "blackness."

FEAST OFFERING (tshogs kyi 'khor lo, tshogs kyi mchod pa; Skt. ganachakra) A tantric ritual connected to the sadhana practice of one of the three roots: guru, yidam, or dakini. *Feast* literally means "gathering": the gathering of enlightened guests, the practitioners, the feast articles, and the two accumulations of merit and wisdom.

FINAL ENLIGHTENMENT (mthar thug gi byang chub) Complete and perfect buddhahood.

FIRST BARDO (bar do dang po) Usually the moment of "ground luminosity."

FIRST LUMINOSITY (dang po'i 'od gsal) The ground luminosity of primordial purity.

FIVE ASPECTS OF TRUE ENLIGHTENMENT (mngon byang lnga) Five aspects of visualization of a deity in the development stage: moon disc, sun disc, seed syllable, symbolic attribute, and the complete form of the deity.

Glossary

FIVE BUDDHA ASPECTS (rgyal ba rigs lnga) *See* five families of jinas.

FIVE BUDDHA FAMILIES (rigs lnga) The families of buddha, vajra, ratna, padma, and karma.

FIVE CHAKRAS ('khor lo lnga) The five nadi-wheels in the vajra body.

FIVE CONSORTS (yum lnga) The five female buddhas.

FIVE ELEMENTS Earth, water, fire, wind, and space.

FIVE FAMILIES (rigs lnga) (1) Same as five families of jinas. (2) Five buddha families.

FIVE FAMILIES OF JINAS (rgyal ba rigs lnga) The buddha aspects: Vairochana, Akshobhya, Ratnasambhava, Amitabha, Amoghasiddhi.

FIVE FEMALE BUDDHAS (rgyal ba yum lnga) Dhatvishvari, Mamaki, Locana, Pandaravasini, Samayatara.

FIVE PATHS (lam lnga) The path of accumulation, joining, seeing, cultivation, and nonlearning. The five paths over the entire process from beginning dharma practice to complete enlightenment.

FIVE POISONOUS KLESHAS (nyon mongs pa dug lnga) The five poisons.

FIVE POISONS (dug lnga) Desire, anger, delusion, arrogance, and envy.

FIVE SENSE CONSCIOUSNESSES (sgo lnga'i rnam shes) The five functions of cognizing the sense objects of visual form, sound, smell, taste, and texture.

FIVE SKANDHAS (phung po lnga) The five aspects which comprise the physical and mental constituents of a sentient being: physical forms, sensations, conceptions, (mental) formations, and consciousnesses.

FIVE SUPERKNOWLEDGES (mngon shes lnga) The capacities for performing miracles, divine sight, divine hearing, recollection of former lives, and cognition of the minds of others.

FIVE TYPES OF NAMJANG (rnam byang lnga) The natural lights of the buddha nature, the basic state of all beings. Depending upon whether the practitioner recognizes that these lights are the expression of his innate essence or grasps them as being phenomena external to himself, he will proceed toward liberation or further entanglement in samsaric existence.

FIVE WISDOMS (ye shes lnga) The dharmadhatu wisdom, mirrorlike wisdom, wisdom of equality, discriminating wisdom, and all-accomplishing wisdom. The five wisdoms should not be understood as being separate or individually achieved entities. Rather, they are different "facets of the same jewel" or the different functions of one's enlightened essence in its naked state.

FOUR ACTIVITIES (las bzhi) Pacifying, increasing, magnetizing, and subjugating.

FOUR CONTINENTS (gling bzhi) The four continents surrounding Mount Sumeru: Superior Body, Jambudvipa, Cow Enjoyment, and Unpleasant Sound. Human beings live on all four continents, but on Unpleasant Sound they are not suitable to practice the buddha dharma.

FOUR EMPOWERMENTS (dbang bzhi) The empowerments of vase, secret, wisdom-knowledge, and precious word according to Anuttara Tantra of the Sarma schools or the Three Inner Tantras of the Nyingma system. The purpose of receiving these empowerments is to be "ripened" so as to be authorized to practice the following four aspects of the vajrayana paths:

By receiving the vase empowerment, one is authorized to practice the development stage, the union of appearance and emptiness, according to the teachings of Mahayoga Tantra.

By receiving the secret empowerment, one is authorized to practice the completion stage with concepts, the profound path, which is the unity of clarity and emptiness connected with the "higher gate" of Anuyoga Tantra.

By receiving the wisdom-knowledge empowerment, one is authorized to practice the completion stage with concepts, the phonya path, which is the union of bliss and emptiness connected to the "lower gate" of Anuyoga Tantra.

By receiving the precious word empowerment, one is authorized to practice the Great Perfection, which is the union of awareness and emptiness connected to Ati Yoga Tantra.

Guru Rinpoche said in his *Lamrim Yeshe Nyingpo:*

The vase empowerment, which purifies the body and the
nadis,

Is the seed of the vajra body and nirmanakaya.

The secret empowerment, which purifies speech and the
pranas,

Is the seed of the vajra speech and samboghyakaya.

The phonya empowerment, which purifies the mind and
the bindus,

Is the seed of the vajra mind and dharmakaya.

The ultimate empowerment, which purifies habitual
patterns and the all-ground,

Is the seed of the vajra wisdom and the svabhavikakaya.

FOUR IMMEASURABLES (tshad med bzhi) Compassion, love, joy,
and impartiality.

FOUR KAYAS (sku bzhi) The three kayas in addition to svabhavikakaya.

FOUR MARAS (bdud bzhi) Lord of Death, Godly Son, Klesha,
and Skandha.

FOUR MEANS OF MAGNETIZING (bsdu ba'i dngos po bzhi)
Generosity, pleasing speech, giving appropriate teachings,
and maintaining consistency in behavior.

FOUR MIND-CHANGINGS (blo ldog rnam bzhi) (1) The freedoms
and riches that are so difficult to find. (2) Impermanence
and death. (3) Karma, the law of cause and effect. (4) The
defects of samsara. Reflecting on these four topics of the
facts of life causes one's mind to change and be directed
toward dharma practice.

FOUR MUDRAS (phyag rgya bzhi) Four aspects of tantric practice.

FOUR SESSIONS (thun bzhi) Dawn, morning, afternoon, and
evening.

FOUR VIDYADHARA LEVELS (rig 'dzin rnam pa bzhi'i go
'phang) *See* Four vidyadharas.

FOUR VIDYADHARAS (rig 'dzin bzhi) The four knowledge-hold-
ers, masters of the four stages of the tantric path of Mahayoga. The four vidyadhara levels are the Fully Matured,

Life-Mastery, Great Seal, and Spontaneously Accomplished (rnam smin, tshe dbang, phyag chen, lhun grub). The Mahayoga equivalent to the ten bodhisattva bhumis.

FOUR VISIONS (snang ba bzhi)   Four stages in Dzogchen practice: manifest dharmata, increased experience, awareness reaching fullness, and exhaustion of concepts and phenomena. The Maha Ati equivalent to the ten bodhisattva bhumis.

FOURTH EMPOWERMENT (dbang bzhi pa)   Also known as the "precious word empowerment" (tshig dbang rin po che). *See* four empowerments.

FREE AND WELL-FAVORED HUMAN FORM (dal 'byor gyi mi lus)   A human existence endowed with the eight freedoms and ten riches.

FRUITION OF UNITY (zung 'jug gi 'bras bu)   Complete enlightenment, the unified level of a vajra holder. *Unity* refers to the union of means and knowledge, appearance and emptiness, or space and awareness. According to Jamyang Khyentse Wangpo, *unity* refers to the unified state of the kayas and wisdoms, in which *kaya* is emptiness endowed with the supreme of all aspects and *wisdom* is the mind of unchanging great bliss.

FULFILLED ACTION (las rab rdzogs pa)   The pure realm of Buddha Amoghasiddhi.

FULLY LIBERATING SAMSARA ('khor ba yongs grol)   The pure realm of Buddha Vairochana.

GARAB DORJE (dga' rab rdo rje, Prahevajra/Pramoda Vajra)   The forefather of the Dzogchen lineage, who received the transmission from Vajrasattva.

GENERAL PRELIMINARIES (thun mong gi sngon 'gro)   The four mind-changings. Through these teachings one's mind will turn toward dharma practice.

GIVING AND TAKING (gtong len)   A bodhicitta practice of giving one's virtue and happiness to others and taking their suffering and misdeeds upon oneself.

GLORIOUS HERUKA (dpal chen he ru ka)   The chief buddha of the fifty-eight wrathful deities.

GOD (lha)   In this context, one of the six classes of beings.

GÖTSANGPA (rgod tshang pa) A great master of the Drukpa Kagyü School.

GRASPING AND FIXATION (gzung 'dzin) Refers to the duality of an object perceived and the mind that perceives it.

GREAT COMPASSIONATE ONE (thugs rje chen po) Avalo-kiteshvara.

GREAT PERFECTION (rdzogs pa chen po, mahasandhi/maha ati) The third of the three inner tantras. Same as Dzogchen.

GREAT SEAL (phyag rgya chen po) Same as Mahamudra.

GREAT UPPER DIRECTNESS (yar gyi zang thal chen po) The attainment of enlightenment without having to go through the intermediate states.

GREATER AND LESSER VEHICLES (theg pa che chung) Mahayana and hinayana.

GROUND LUMINOSITY (gzhi'i 'od gsal) Synonymous with *mother luminosity*.

GROUND LUMINOSITY OF THE FIRST BARDO (bar do dang po gzhi'i 'od gsal) Synonymous with *mother luminosity*.

GROUND LUMINOSITY OF THE NATURAL STATE (gnas lugs gzhi'i 'od gsal) Synonymous with *mother luminosity*.

GUHYAMANTRA (gsang sngags) Synonymous with *vajrayana* or *tantric teachings*. *Guhya* means secret, both concealed and self-secret. *Mantra* in this context means eminent, excellent, or praiseworthy. Same as *Secret Mantra*.

GURU (bla ma) Spiritual teacher, especially a vajrayana master.

GURU RINPOCHE (guru rin po che) The essence of all the buddhas of the three times, the supreme sovereign of all power-wielding vidyadharas, the all-encompassing lord of the ocean of peaceful and wrathful yidams, the chief of the gatherings of all the dakas and dakinis, the great being who by his splendor outshines all the vajra protectors of the dharma and the haughty forces of the phenomenal realm, is the one known as Mahaguru Padmasambhava throughout the infinite realms of the teachers of the three kayas.

Invited by Manjushri's incarnation, the dharma-upholding king Trisong Detsen, he came to this snowy land of

Tibet, the realm of the noble Great Compassionate One. He put all the vicious elemental forces under the majestic seal of his command, erected the triple-styled Unchanging and Spontaneously Perfected Temple, a palace with shrines, and strew the flowers of consecration. He established the great tradition of expounding and practicing the entire doctrine of the Buddha, and in particular he turned an infinite variety of the dharma-wheels of the tantras, texts, and instructions of vajrayana.

He visited personally all the sacred places—the snow mountains, caves, and lakes—blessed them, and concealed innumerable named and unnamed treasures. Thus his immeasurable kindness permeates the entire land of Tibet, both the central and the surrounding lands, and will remain right up to the last of the final days in the future. Samaya.

GYALWA YANG GÖNPA (rgyal ba yang dgon pa) A master of the Drukpa Kagyü School.

GYÜBUM (rgyud 'bum) The Hundred Thousand Tantras of the Nyingma School.

HASHANG VIEW (ha shang gi lta ba) The view propagated in Tibet by Chinese Buddhist masters. When used in a negative sense it means to simply pursue a meditative state devoid of conceptual thinking, that is, lacking the clarity of discriminating knowledge.

HEARING LINEAGE (nyan brgyud) The lineage of oral teachings from master to disciple.

HERUKA (he ru ka, khrag 'thung) In this context, the wrathful or semiwrathful male deities appearing to one in the bardo of dharmata.

HEVAJRA TANTRA (kye rdo rje'i rgyud) A tantra of anuttara yoga.

HUNDRED SACRED ASPECTS (dam pa rigs brgya) The forty-two peaceful and fifty-eight wrathful deities.

IGNORANT ASPECT OF THE ALL-GROUND (kun gzhi ma rig pa'i cha) Synonymous with *coemergent ignorance*.

ILLUSORY BODY (sgyu lus) One of the Six Doctrines of Naropa.

INCREASE (mched pa)   The second of the three experience of appearance, increase, and attainment.

INCREASED EXPERIENCE (nyams snang gong 'phel)   The second of the four visions in Dzogchen practice.

INNER PATH OF VAJRASTTVA (rdo rje sems dpa' khong seng gi lam)   One of the last experiences in the bardo of dharmata.

INNERMOST UNEXCELLED CYCLE OF NYINGTHIG (yang gsang bla na med pa'i snying thig gi skor)   The fourth of the four divisions of the Instruction Section of Dzogchen according to the arrangement of Shri Singha. See Appendix.

INSTRUCTION SECTION (man ngag gi sde)   The third of the three sections of Dzogchen as arranged by Jampal Shenyen.

INTERMEDIATE EXISTENCE (bar ma do'i srid pa)   In general, the period between dying and the next rebirth.

JAMBUDVIPA ('dzam bu gling)   The southern of the four continents surrounding Mount Sumeru. The term usually refers to our known world.

JAMPAL SHENYEN ('jam dpal bshes gnyen)   Manjushrimitra (Skt.), a great Indian pandita who became the chief disciple of Garab Dorje. According to the historical scriptures, Manjushrimitra was a highly respected scholar at Nalanda Buddhist University in India. The fame of Garab Dorje as a proponent of a new system transcending cause and effect (i.e., the causal vehicles) reached Nalanda, and the panditas were outraged. They would not permit such a heretic to misguide people and sent a delegation to refute Garab Dorje, who lived in the kingdom of Uddiya to the northwest of Bodhgaya. Manjushrimitra confronted Garab Dorje and tried to defeat him in debate but failed. Now, with trust in the teachings beyond effort, cause, and effect, Manjushrimitra felt strong remorse at having tried to defeat the Great Perfection and wanted to cut off his own tongue in order to prevent further misdeeds. Garab Dorje read his mind and said, "You can purify your obscuration if you cause the correct Dzogchen teachings to flourish in this world, but not by cutting off your tongue even a thousand times." Manjushrimitra then composed the treatise known as *Gomnyam Drukpa,* "Six Experiences of Meditation," and upheld the system of the Great Perfection. Later, his level of realization became equal to that of Garab Dorje.

JINA (rgyal ba) Victorious One. A buddha; one who has conquered the four Maras.

JINA MANDALAS (rgyal ba'i dkyil 'khor) The mandalas of the five buddhas.

JNANASUTRA (ye shes mdo) An Indian master in the early Dzogchen lineage who was a disciple of Shri Singha. A close dharma friend and later teacher of Vimalamitra.

JONANGPA (jo nang pa) Another name for Jetsun Taranatha.

JORDRUK (sbyor drug) One of the Eight Practice Lineages. Literally, "Six Unions," according to the system of Kalachakra.

KALACHAKRA (dus kyi 'khor lo) A tantra and a vajrayana system taught by Buddha Shakyamuni and later preserved in the kingdom of Shambhala.

KAMA (bka' ma) The Oral Lineage of the Nyingma School, transmitted from master to student, of the body of teachings translated chiefly during the period of Guru Rinpoche's stay in Tibet.

KANGYUR (bka' 'gyur) The "Translated Words" of Buddha Shakyamuni. The Buddhist canon of about 108 volumes of scriptures.

KARMA (las) *Karma* literally means "action." In a general sense, it is the law of cause and effect, ruling that positive actions bring happiness and misdeeds yield suffering. Only through realizing selflessness and emptiness does one transcend the karma of cyclic existence, after which all activities are "undefiled" and result in manifesting the nirmanakayas for the benefit of beings.

KARMA FAMILY (las kyi rigs) One of the five families.

KARMA-MUDRA (las kyi phyag rgya) One of the four mudras.

KARMAS AND KLESHAS (las dang nyon mongs pa) These two comprise the truth of origin among the four noble truths.

KARMIC BARDO OF BECOMING (srid pa las kyi bar do) The period from emerging in a mental body until entering a womb at the moment of conception.

KAYA (sku) *Kaya* literally means "body" in the sense of "embodiment of numerous qualities." Thus dharmakaya, for instance, is the "body" of all enlightened wisdom "qualities," such as the ten powers and the fourfold fearlessness.

KAYAS AND WISDOMS (sku dang ye shes) The four kayas and five wisdoms.

KHACHÖ (mkha' spyod) The accomplishment of being able to go to a celestial realm. Can also refer to the pure realm of Vajra Yogini.

KLESHAS OF THE FIVE POISONS (dug lnga'i nyon mongs pa) *See* five poisons.

KLESHAS (nyon mongs pa) Disturbing emotions. *See* five poisons.

KRIYA (bya ba [rgyud]) The first of the three outer tantras.

KRIYA, CHARYA, AND YOGA TANTRAS (bya rgyud, spyod rgyud, rnal 'byor rgyud) The three outer tantras among the nine vehicles.

KYOTÖN SÖNAM LAMA (skyo ston bsod nams bla ma) The root teacher of Machik Labdrön.

LAMDRE (lam 'bras) Path and Fruition/Result. The main teaching of the Sakya School.

LAND OF SNOW (gangs can gyi yul) Tibet.

LATER TRANSLATION SCHOOLS (phyi 'gyur) Sarma, the New Schools, composed of Kagyu, Sakya, and Gelug.

LEVEL OF OMNISCIENCE (thams cad mkhyen pa) Complete buddhahood.

LIBERATION (thar pa) Emancipation from samsara.

LIBERATION AND OMNISCIENCE (thar pa dang thams cad mkhyen pa) Refers to liberation from samsaric existence and the state of complete enlightenment.

LIFE-POWER VIDYADHARA (tshe dbang rig 'dzin) The second of the four vidyadhara levels.

LOJONG (blo sbyong) Mind Training. The mahayana meditation system of the early Kadampa School as brought to Tibet by Atisha Dipamkara.

LONG LINEAGE OF KAMA (ring brgyud bka' ma) *See* Kama.

Glossary

LONGCHENPA (klong chen pa) Great Nyingma master and writer.

LORD NAGARJUNA (mgon po klu grub) *See* Acharya Nagarjuna.

LORD OF DEATH (gshin rje) A personification of impermanence and the unfailing law of cause and effect.

LOTUS MOUND (pad ma brtsegs pa) The pure realm of Buddha Amitabha.

LUMINOSITY DISSOLVING INTO UNION ('od gsal zung 'jug la thim pa) One of the dissolution stages during the bardo of dharmata.

LUMINOSITY MANIFESTATIONS OF SPONTANEOUS PRESENCE (lhun grub 'od gsal gyi snang ba) The display during the bardo of dharmata.

LUMINOSITY OF APPEARANCE (snang ba'i 'od gsal) The first of the three stages of appearance, increase, and attainment.

LUMINOSITY OF THE FIRST BARDO (bar do dang po'i od gsal) Same as *mother luminosity*.

LUMINOSITY ('od gsal). Literally, "free from darkness of unknowing and endowed with the ability to cognize." There are the two aspects of "empty luminosity" like a clear open sky and "apparent luminosity" like five-colored lights, images, and so forth.

LUMINOUS BARDO OF DHARMATA (chos nyid 'od gsal gyi bar do) The period from the moment after death until one emerges in the mental body of the bardo of becoming.

LUMINOUS DHARMAKAYA ('od gsal chos kyi sku) *See* Dharmakaya.

LUMINOUS HEART ESSENCE ('od gsal rdo rje snying po) The Instruction Section of Dzogchen. See Appendix.

LUNG ANU YOGA (lung anu yoga) The second of the three inner tantras, emphasizing the completion stage.

MACHIK LABDRÖN (ma gcig lab sgron) The great female master who set down the Chöd practice.

MADHYAMIKA (dbu ma) The Middle [Way]. The highest Mahayana school of philosophy.

Glossary

MAHA [rnal 'byor] chen po). The first of the three inner tantras. The emphasis of this tantra is the buddha-mandala as the pure aspect of oneself, the people, and the environment. The chief practice is the development stage.

MAHA ATI (rdzogs chen) The third of the three inner tantras. For the most part synonymous with Dzogchen.

MAHAMUDRA (phyag rgya chen po) A system of teachings which is the basic view of vajrayana practice according to the Sarma schools.

MANDALA (dkyil 'khor) Literally, "center and surrounding," but the term should be understood according to context. Usually a deity along with its surrounding environment.

MANIFEST DHARMATA (chos nyid mngon sum) The first of the four visions in Dzogchen practice.

MANJUSHRIMITRA ('jam dpal bshes gnyen) An Indian master of the Dzogchen lineage and a disciple of Garab Dorje. Same as Jampal Shenyen.

MANTRAYANA (sngags kyi theg pa) Secret mantra or vajrayana.

MANTRIKA (sngags pa) A practitioner of vajrayana.

MARKS AND SIGNS (mtshan dpe) The thirty-two major and eighty minor marks of excellence of a perfect buddha.

MARPA (mar pa) The great Tibetan master and disciple of Naropa who brought the teachings of Mahamudra and the Six Doctrines to Tibet. See *The Life of Marpa the Translator* (Shambhala Publications, 1982).

MELONG DORJE (me long rdo rje) A great Tibetan master in the Oral Lineage of the Nyingma School.

MIDDLE (dbu ma) Madhyamika.

MILAREPA (mi la ras pa) A great Tibetan master and the chief disciple of Marpa. See *The Life of Milarepa* (Shambhala Publications, 1977).

MIND AND SPACE SECTIONS (sems sde, klong sde) The first two of the three sections of Dzogchen.

MIND CONSCIOUSNESS (yid kyi rnam par shes pa) One of the eight consciousnesses according to abhidharma. It is the function of discriminating and labeling things.

Glossary

MIND SECTION OF DZOGCHEN (rdzogs chen sems sde)   The first of the three sections of Dzogchen.

MIND TRAINING (blo sbyong)   *See* Lojong.

MIRRORLIKE WISDOM (me long lta bu'i ye shes)   One of the five wisdoms.

MOTHER LUMINOSITY (ma'i 'od gsal)   The ground luminosity of the natural state, inherent as the enlightened essence of all sentient beings.

NADI (rtsa)   The channels in the vajra body through which the winds (prana) flow.

NADI-KNOTS (rtsa mdud).   Symbolic term for defilements in the channels of the vajra body, preventing the free flow of the pranas.

NADI-WHEEL (rtsa 'khor)   Generally, the four or five "wheels" or chakras in the body.

NAGARJUNA (klu grub)   An Indian master of philosophy. *See* Acharya Nagarjuna.

NAGI GOMPA (na gi dgon pa)   The hermitage near Kathmandu where Tulku Urgyen Rinpoche resides.

NAMJANG (rnam byang)   "Complete perfection." In this context the term specifically refers to the natural light of the enlightened essence of mind.

NAMO GURU (bla ma la phyag 'tshal lo)   Homage to the master!

NAROPA (na ro pa)   The chief disciple of Tilopa and the guru of Marpa in the Kagyü Lineage.

NATURAL BARDO OF THIS LIFE (rang bzhin skye gnas kyi bar do)   *See* bardo of this life.

NATURAL FACE (rang zhal)   The nature of mind.

NATURAL NIRMANAKAYA (rang bzhin sprul sku)   The pure nirmanakaya realms manifested by the buddhas of the five families, such as the realm of Sukhavati.

NATURAL NIRMANAKAYA REALM (rang bzhin sprul pa sku'i zhing)   The emanated realms of the five buddhas.

NATURAL SOUND OF DHARMATA (chos nyid kyi rang sgra)   One of the experiences during the bardo of dharmata. The innate vajra speech of the buddha nature.

Glossary

NEW AND OLD SCHOOLS (gsar rnying) The New Schools are Kagyü, Sakya, and Gelug. The Old School refers to the Nyingma.

NIHILISM (chad lta) Literally, "the view of discontinuance." The extreme view of nothingness: no rebirth or karmic effects, and the nonexistence of a mind after death.

NIRMANAKAYA (sprul pa'i sku) "Emanation body." The third of the three kayas.

NIRVANA (mya ngan las 'das pa) The lesser nirvana refers to the liberation from cyclic existence attained by a hinayana practitioner. When referring to a buddha, *nirvana* is the great nondwelling state of enlightenment which falls neither into the extreme of samsaric existence nor into the passive state of cessation attained by an arhant.

NOBLE AND ORDINARY BEINGS ('phags pa dang so so skye bo) The "noble" or "exalted" beings are great masters, bodhisattvas, or arhants who have attained the path of seeing the third of the five paths. Ordinary beings are all others before reaching the path of seeing.

NOBLE LAND ('phags yul) India.

NOBLE ONES ('phags pa) *See* noble and ordinary beings.

NONAPPARENT LUMINOSITY (snag med 'od gsal) The luminosity of dharmakaya or empty luminosity.

NYANG BEN TINGDZIN SANGPO (nyang dben ting 'dzin bzang po) A close disciple of Vimalamitra and Guru Rinpoche. He later incarnated as the great tertön Jatson Nyingpo, one of Tsele Natsok Rangdröl's teachers.

NYIME NAMGYAL (gnyis med rnam rgyal) A tantric scripture.

NYINGMA SCHOOL (rnying ma) The teachings brought to Tibet and translated chiefly during the reign of King Trisong Detsen and in the following period up to Rinchen Sangpo. The two principal types of teaching are kama and terma.

OBJECTS OF REFUGE (skyabs yul) The three jewels, three roots, and three kayas.

OBSCURATION OF CONCEPTUAL KNOWLEDGE (shes bya'i sgrib pa) The subtle obscuration of holding on to the concepts of subject, object, and action.

Glossary

OLD SCHOOL OF THE EARLY TRANSLATIONS (snga 'gyur rnying ma) *See* Nyingma School.

OMNISCIENCE (rnam mkhyen, thams cad mkhyen pa) Complete enlightenment or buddhahood.

ONE INSTANT OF COMPLETED ACTION (bya rdzogs kyi skad gcig ma) A short moment such as a finger-snap or a long period such as from initially engendering bodhicitta until final and complete buddhahood.

ORAL LINEAGE (bka' ma) *See* Kama.

ORGYEN (o rgyan) Same as Guru Rinpoche.

ORGYEN RINPOCHE (o rgyan rin po che) Same as Guru Rinpoche.

OUTER AND INNER TANTRA SECTIONS (phyi nang gi rgyud sde) The three outer are kriya, upa, and yoga. The three inner are maha, anu, and ati.

PACIFIER (zhi byed) *See* Shije.

PADMA (pad ma) Same as Guru Rinpoche.

PADMAKARA (pad ma 'byung gnas) "Lotus-born." Same as Guru Rinpoche.

PAINFUL BARDO OF DYING ('chi kha sdug bsngal gyi bar do) *See* bardo of dying.

PANDITA (mkhas pa) A learned master or scholar.

PATH AND FRUITION (lam 'bras) *See* Lamdre.

PATH AND RESULT (lam 'bras) *See* Lamdre.

PATH OF MEANS (thabs lam) Here the term refers to the practices of the Six Doctrines. It should be practiced in combination with the path of liberation, which is Mahamudra itself.

PATH OF THE TWO STAGES (rim gnyis kyi lam) The two stages of development and completion, which are the means and knowledge (prajna and upaya) of vajrayana practice.

PATHS (lam) The five paths or stages on the way to enlightenment: the path of accumulation, joining, seeing, cultivation, and no learning.

PATHS AND BHUMIS (sa lam) The five paths and the ten bodhisattva levels.

PEACEFUL AND WRATHFUL ONES (zhi khro)   The forty-two peaceful and fifty-eight wrathful divinities.

PEACEFUL DEITIES OF VAJRADHATU (zhi ba rdo rje dbyings kyi lha tshogs)   The forty-two peaceful deities: Samantabhadra and Samantabhadri, the five male and female buddhas, the eight male and female bodhisattvas, the six munis, and the four male and female gatekeepers.

PERFECT RECALL (mi brjed pa'i gzungs)   A perfect memory, the essence of which is nondistraction.

PERSONAL EXPERIENCE (rang snang)   The example for this is the dream experience. Sometimes this term has been translated as "one's own projection" or "self-display."

PHADAMPA (pha dam pa)   The Indian mahasiddha who brought the Shije (zhi byed) teachings to Tibet.

PHOWA ('pho ba)   Ejection of consciousness to a buddha-field at the moment of death.

PHOWA OF THE CELESTIAL REALM (mkha' spyod 'pho ba)   A type of phowa.

PRACTICE LINEAGE (sgrub brgyud)   The lineage of masters where the emphasis is one's personal experience of the teachings, as opposed to the scholastic lineage of expounding the scriptures (bshad brgyud). *See* Eight Practice Lineages.

PRAHEVAJRA (dga' rab rdo rje)   The human recipient of the maha ati teachings. *See* Garab Dorje.

PRAJNAPARAMITA (shes rab kyi pha rol tu phyin pa)   "Transcendent knowledge." The mahayana teachings on insight into emptiness.

PRANA (rlung)   The "winds" or energy-currents of the vajra body.

PRANA-MIND (rlung sems)   *Prana* here is the "wind of karma," and *mind* is the dualistic consciousness of an unenlightened being.

PRATIMOKSHA (so so thar pa)   "Individual Liberation," the seven sets of precepts for ordained and lay people according to the vinaya.

PRATYEKABUDDHA (rang sangs rgyas)   A person who has reached perfection in the second hinayana vehicle.

PRECIOUS BUDDHA (sangs rgyas dkon mchog) The state of buddhahood endowed with the perfect benefit for self and others.

PRECIOUS DHARMA (chos dkon mchog) The truth consisting of scripture and realization.

PRECIOUS ONES (dkon mchog) The three jewels.

PRECIOUS REALMS OF SPONTANEOUS PRESENCE (lhun grub rin po che'i zhing) One of the last experiences in the bardo of dharmata.

PRECIOUS SANGHA (dge 'dun dkon mchog) Noble and accomplished practitioners endowed with the virtues of knowledge and liberation.

PRECIOUS SPHERE (rin po che'i sbubs) Same as "precious realms of spontaneous presence."

PRIMORDIAL PROTECTOR (mdod ma'i mgon po) The originally enlightened one, Adibuddha, Samantabhadra.

PRIMORDIAL PURITY (ka dag) The basic nature of sentient beings, which is originally untainted by defilement, beyond confusion and liberation.

PROFOUND AND EXTENSIVE TEACHINGS (zab rgyas kyi chos) Same as sutra and mantra.

PROFOUND PATH (zab lam) Refers here to the Mahamudra teachings.

PURE ILLUSORY BODY (dag pa sgyu lus) The form of a deity.

RAINBOW BODY ('ja' lus) At the time of death of a practitioner who has reached the exhaustion of all grasping and fixation through the Dzogchen practice of Thögal, the five gross elements which form the physical body dissolve back into their essences, five-colored light (the natural lights of the buddha nature). Sometimes only the hair and the nails are left behind.

RATNA FAMILY (rin chen gyi rigs) One of the five buddha families.

RATNASAMBHAVA (rin chen 'byung gnas) One of the five buddha aspects.

RECOGNITION (ngo shes, ngo 'phrod) In this context, recognition of the nature of one's mind. See the introductory discourse by Tulku Urgyen Rinpoche.

REDNESS (dmar lam) The second stage of the subtle dissolution stages of appearance, increase, and attainment.

REFUGE (skyabs 'gro) Placing one's confidence in the precious ones, the three jewels.

REMINDING-INSTRUCTION (gsal 'debs) Refers here to the pointing-out instruction for recognizing the nature of mind, repeated for a practitioner at the verge of death by a master or a close dharma friend.

REPRESENTATIONS OF BODY, SPEECH, AND MIND (sku gsung thugs rten) These are, for example, statues, scriptures, and stupas.

RIPENED AND FREED (smin grol) *See* Ripening and liberation.

RIPENING AND LIBERATION (smin grol) Ripening through empowerment and liberation through oral instruction.

ROOT GURU (rtsa we'i bla ma) The general root guru is the vajra master from whom one receives empowerment and explanation of the tantric teachings. The specific root guru is the master who points out the nature of mind.

RUPAKAYA (gzugs sku) The "form body" composed of sambhogakaya and nirmanakaya.

RUPAKAYA OF SPONTANEOUS PRESENCE (lhun grub kyi gzugs sku) The display of the bardo of dharmata.

SADHANA (sgrub thabs) Tantric liturgy and procedure for practice, usually emphasizing the development stage.

SAMANTABHADRA (kun tu bzang po) The primordial dharmakaya buddha.

SAMANTABHADRI (kun tu bzang mo) The consort of Samantabhadra.

SAMAYA (dam tshig) The sacred pledge or commitment of vajrayana practice. There are many details, but essentially the samayas consist of, outwardly, keeping a harmonious relationship with the vajra master and one's dharma friends and, inwardly, not straying from the continuity of the practice.

SAMAYA-MUDRA (dam tshig gi phyag rgya) One of the four mudras.

SAMBHOGAKAYA (longs spyod rdzogs pa'i sku)   The "body of perfect enjoyment." One of the three, four, or five kayas. The sambhogakaya should be understood in terms of ground, path, and fruition. The sambhogakaya of ground is the mind's innate capacity for knowing. The sambhogakaya of path is that as well as the luminous nature of bliss, clarity, and nonthought. The sambhogakaya of fruition is defined as the five perfections: The perfect teacher is the fully enlightened buddha in a rainbow body adorned with the thirty-two major and eighty minor marks of excellence. The perfect retinue is the bodhisattvas on the ten bhumis. The perfect place is the pure realms of the five families. The perfect teaching is Mahayana and Vajrayana. The perfect time is the "perpetual circle of continuity."

SAMBHOGAKAYA LUMINOSITY (longs sku'i 'od gsal)   The luminosity during the bardo of dharmata.

SAMSARA ('khor ba)   Cyclic existence.

SARMA (gsar ma)   *See* New Schools.

SARMA SCHOOLS OF SECRET MANTRA (gsang sngags gsar ma) *See* New Schools.

SECRET CYCLE OF LUMINOSITY ('od gsal gsang skor)   An aspect of the Instruction Section of Dzogchen.

SECRET EMPOWERMENT (gsang ba'i dbang)   The second of the four empowerments.

SECRET MANTRA (gsang sngags, guhyamantra)   Vajrayana. *See* Guhyamantra.

SECRET MANTRA OF THE GREATER VEHICLE (theg pa chen po'i gsang sngags)   Vajrayana when regarded as a part of mahayana.

SEVEN ASPECTS OF UNION (kha sbyor yan lag bdun)   The seven qualities of a sambhogakaya buddha: complete enjoyment, union, great bliss, absence of a self-nature, presence of compassion, being uninterrupted, and unceasing.

SEVEN KINDS OF VOWS OF THE PRATIMOKSHA (so so thar pa'i ris bdun)   Seven sets of vows for ordained monks and nuns, novices, and lay people.

SHAKYAMUNI (sha kya thub pa)   Buddha Shakyamuni, the historical Buddha.

Glossary

SHAMATHA (zhi gnas)   Calm abiding, the meditative practice of calming the mind in order to rest free from the disturbance of thought activity. For details see Dakpo Tashi Namgyal's *Mahamudra* (Shambhala Publications, 1986).

SHIJE (zhi byed)   Pacifying, one of the Eight Practice Lineages brought to Tibet by Phadampa Sangye.

SHORT LINEAGE OF TERMA (nye brgyud gter ma)   The Dharma treasures concealed chiefly by Guru Rinpoche to be discovered in the future by a tertön, a treasure revealer.

SHRAVAKA (nyan thos)   A hinayana follower of the Buddha.

SHRI SINGHA   A master in the Dzogchen lineage and root guru of Guru Rinpoche. Shri Singha attained complete realization of the Dzogchen teachings and, along with Gura Rinpoche, was one of the only two masters to fully attain the "empowerment of the display of awareness," through which they could transform the phenomenal world in any way they desired.

SIDDHA (grub thob)   An accomplished master.

SIDDHIS (dngos grub)   The supreme and common accomplishments. The supreme siddhi is the attainment of complete enlightenment. The common siddhis are usually eight types of miraculous powers.

SIGN LUMINOSITY (brda'i 'od gsal)   The experiences of manifest luminosity during the bardo of dying.

SIX CLASSES OF BEINGS ('gro ba rigs drug)   Gods, demigods, human beings, animals, hungry ghosts, and hell beings.

SIX DOCTRINES (chos drug)   Tummo, illusory body, dream, luminosity, bardo, and phowa.

SIX LAMPS (sgron ma drug)   A key term in Thögal practice, Connected to the Innermost Unexcelled Cycle of the Great Perfection.

SIX MILLION TANTRAS (rgyud 'bum phrag drug cu)   The tantras of Dzogchen received by Garab Dorje from Vajrasattva.

SIX PARAMITAS (phar phyin drug)   The six transcendent actions of generosity, discipline, patience, diligence, concentration, and discriminating knowledge.

Glossary

SIX REALMS (gnas ris drug) The realms of the six classes of beings.

SIX RECOLLECTIONS (rjes dran drug) There are different lists, of which the most appropriate is as follows: recollection of the yidam deity, the path, the place of rebirth, the meditative state, the oral instructions of the teacher, and the view.

SIX SYLLABLES (yi ge drug pa) The mantra of Avalokiteshvara: OM MANI PADME HUNG.

SIX TANTRA SECTIONS (rgyud sde drug) The three outer tantras of kriya, charya, and yoga and the three inner tantras of maha, anu, and ati.

SIX UNIONS (sbyor drug) See Jordruk.

SOUNDS, COLORS, AND LIGHTS (sgra 'od zer gsum) The first manifestations in the bardo of dharmata. They belong to the category of unconditional phenomena.

SPACE DISSOLVING IN LUMINOSITY (nam mkha' 'od gsal la thim pa) The dividing point between the bardo of dying and the bardo of dharmata.

SPECIAL PRELIMINARIES (thun min gyi sngon 'gro) The refuge, bodhicitta, Vajrasattva mantra, mandala offering, and guru yoga.

SPLENDOROUS REALM (dpal dang ldan pa) The buddha-field of Ratnasambhava.

SPONTANEOUS SOUND OF DHARMATA (chos nyid kyi rang sgra) One of the first displays in the bardo of dharmata.

SPONTANEOUSLY PRESENT LUMINOSITY OF THE RUPAKAYAS (gzugs sku lhun grub kyi 'od gsal) The display during the bardo of dharmata.

STAGES OF DEVELOPMENT AND COMPLETION (bskyed rdzogs kyi rim pa) The two main aspects of vajrayana practice.

STATEMENTS AND REALIZATION (lung rtogs) The authoritative scriptures and the realization of the dharma in the minds of noble beings. They are the two qualities of the Precious Dharma.

SUFFERING OF CHANGE ('gyur ba'i sdug bsngal) Mainly the suffering of the three higher realms.

SUFFERING UPON SUFFERING (sdug bsngal gyi sdug bsngal) Mainly the suffering of the three lower realms.

Glossary

SUGATA (bde bar gshegs pa)   A buddha.

SUGATA-ESSENCE (bde gshegs snying po)   Another word for buddha-nature, the enlightened essence inherent in all sentient beings.

SUGATAGARBHA (bde gshegs snying po)   The buddha nature.

SUKHAVATI (bde ba can)   The pure realm of Buddha Amitabha.

SUMERU (ri rab)   The mountain in the center of the four continents.

SUMMIT OF EXISTENCE (srid pa'i rtse mo)   The highest of the four formless realms. Also known as dwelling on the idea "neither absence nor presence of perception."

SUPERIOR BODY (lus 'phags po).   The eastern continent.

SUPREME AND COMMON SIDDHIS (mchog dang thun mong gi dngos grub)   Enlightenment and mundane accomplishments.

SUPREME SIDDHI (mchog gi dngos grub)   The state of complete enlightenment.

SUTRA AND MANTRA (mdo sngags)   *Sutra* refers to the teachings of both hinayana and mahayana. *Mantra* refers to vajrayana.

SUTRA AND TANTRA (mdo rgyud)   Synonymous with *sutra* and *mantra*.

SUTRAS (mdo)   The discourses and teachings given by Buddha Shakyamuni.

SVABHAVIKAKAYA (ngo bo nyid kyi sku)   The "essence body." Sometimes counted as the fourth kaya. It is the unity of the first three.

SYMBOL, MEANING, AND SIGN (brda' don rtags gsum)   Three aspects of vajrayana teachings. For example, the *symbol* is the peaceful and wrathful deities depicted on painted scrolls, made by human beings; the *meaning* they symbolize is the enlightened qualities inherent within our buddha nature; the *sign* is that they naturally manifest to the dead person during the bardo of dharmata.

SYMBOLIC ATTRIBUTE (brda' rtags)   For example, a vajra or a wheel.

TANTRAS (rgyud)   The vajrayana teachings given by the Buddha in his sambhogakaya form.

Glossary

TANTRAS, TEXTS, AND INSTRUCTIONS (rgyud lung man ngag) The term refers here to the teachings of Maha Yoga, Anu Yoga, and Ati Yoga respectively.

TANTRIC SAMAYAS OF THE VIDYADHARAS (rig 'dzin sngags kyi dam tshig) The commitments of a vajrayana practitioner. *See* samaya.

TANTRIC SECTIONS (rgyud sde) The four or six sections of tantras.

TASHI TSERINGMA (bkra shis tshe ring ma) A female dharma protector of Tibet.

TATHAGATA (de bzhin gshegs pa) A fully enlightened buddha.

TEN BHUMIS (sa bcu) The ten bodhisattva levels. For details, see *The Jewel Ornament of Liberation* by sGam.po.pa (Shambhala Publications, 1986).

TEN RICHES ('byor ba bcu) The five riches from others are as follows: a buddha appears, teaches the dharma, the teachings remain, there are followers, and there are teachers with the kindness to teach. The five riches from oneself are: to be a human being, to be born in a central country, having the physical and mental faculties intact, not having a perverted livelihood, and having trust in the three jewels.

TERMA (gter ma) The transmission through concealed treasures hidden, mainly by Guru Rinpoche and Yeshe Tsogyal for the benefit of future disciples.

THÖGAL (thod rgal) "Direct Crossing." One of the two main aspects of Dzogchen practice, the other being Trekchö.

THREE EXCELLENCIES (dam pa gsum) The excellent beginning of bodhicitta, the excellent main part of nonconceptualization, and the excellent conclusion of dedicating the merit. These three aspects should be part of any spiritual practice one does.

THREE JEWELS (dkon mchog gsum) The precious buddha, the precious dharma, and the precious sangha. For a detailed discussion see Thrangu Rinpoche's *Buddha Nature* (Rangjung Yeshe Publications, 1988).

THREE KAYAS (sku gsum) Dharmakaya, sambhogakaya, and nirmanakaya.

THREE MYSTERIES (gsang ba gsum)   The vajra body, speech, and mind.

THREE POISONS (dug gsum)   Attachment, anger, and delusion.

THREE PRECIOUS ONES (dkon mchog gsum)   The Precious Buddha, Dharma, and Sangha.

THREE REALMS (khams gsum)   The samsaric realms of Desire, Form, and Formlessness.

THREE RITUALS (cho ga gsum)   Three steps in visualization of a deity: seat with seed syllable, attribute, and deity.

THREE ROOTS (rtsa ba gsum)   Guru, yidam, and dakini. The Guru is the root of blessings, the Yidam of accomplishment, and the dakini of activity.

THREE SECRETS (gsang ba gsum)   *See* Three mysteries.

THREE SECTIONS (sde gsum)   The three divisions of Dzogchen: Mind Section, Space Section, and Instruction Section.

THREE SETS OF PRECEPTS (sdom gsum)   *See* Three vows.

THREE TRAININGS (bslab pa gsum)   The trainings of discipline, samadhi, and discriminating knowledge.

THREE VEHICLES (theg pa gsum)   Hinayana, mahayana, and vajrayana.

THREE VOWS (sdom pa gsum)   The hinayana vows of individual liberation, the mahayana trainings of a bodhisattva, and the vajrayana samayas of a vidyadhara.

THREE WORLDS ('jig rten gsum)   The three spheres of gods, humans, and nagas.

THREE YOGAS (rnal 'byor gsum)   In this book, the three inner tantras.

THREE-THOUSANDFOLD WORLD SYSTEM (stong gsum gyi 'jig rten gyi khams)   The world system of Mount Sumeru and the four continents multiplied a thousand times a thousand times a thousand, adding up to one billion.

THREEFOLD EXCELLENCE (dam pa gsum)   The excellent beginning of bodhicitta, the excellent main part of nonconceptualization, and the excellent conclusion of dedication. Also called the three excellencies.

THREEFOLD FAITH (dad pa gsum)   Admiring, yearning, and trusting faith.

Glossary

TILOPA Indian mahasiddha, the guru of Naropa and father of the Kagyü lineage.

TRANSCENDENT KNOWLEDGE (shes rab kyi pha rol tu phyin pa, prajnaparamita) Intelligence that has transcended conceptual thinking.

TREASURE LINEAGES (gter brgyud) The transmission of teachings, hidden as treasures, to be revealed in the future to destined students by a tertön, treasure-revealer.

TREATISES (bstan bcos, shastra) Scriptures composed by accomplished or learned masters.

TREKCHÖ (khregs chod, cutting through) One of the two main aspects of Dzogchen practice, the other being Thögal.

TRIPITAKA (sde snod gsum) The three collections of teachings: vinaya, sutra, and abhidharma.

TRUE JOY (mngon par dga' ba) The pure realm of Buddha Akshobhya.

TRUE LUMINOSITY (don gyi 'od gsal) Empty luminosity.

TRUE MEANING (nges don) The definitive meaning as opposed to the expedient or relative meaning.

TRULY HIGH (mngon mtho) The three higher realms.

TSOGYAL (mtsho rgyal) Khandro Yeshe Tsogyal, the close disciple of Guru Rinpoche who compiled the major part of his teachings.

TULKU URGYEN RINPOCHE (sprul sku u rgyan rin po che) A contemporary master of the Kagyü and Nyingma lineages, who lives at Nagi Gompa in Nepal.

TUMMO (gtum mo, chandali) One of the Six Doctrines of Naropa.

TWELVE LINKS OF INTERDEPENDENCE (rten 'brel yan lag bcu gnyis) Ignorance, formation, consciousness, name-and-form, the six sense bases, contact, sensation, craving, grasping, becoming, rebirth, old age, and death. These twelve links are like an uninterrupted vicious circle, a wheel that spins all sentient beings around and around through the realms of samsara.

TWENTY-FIVE PANDITAS (mkhas pa nyer lnga) Twenty-five masters in the Dzogchen lineage from Garab Dorje to Guru Rinpoche, Vimalamitra, and Vairochana.

Glossary

TWO ACCUMULATIONS (tshogs gnyis) The accumulation of merit and of wisdom.

TWO KAYAS (sku gnyis) Dharmakaya and rupakaya.

TWO PROFOUND STAGES (zab mo'i rim pa gnyis) The development stage and the completion stage.

TWO STAGES (rim gnyis) The two profound stages.

TWOFOLD PURITY (dag pa gnyis) Inherent or primordial purity and the purity of having removed all temporary obscurations.

ULTIMATE TRANSCENDENT KNOWLEDGE (don dam shes rab kyi pha rol tu phyin pa) See transcendent knowledge.

ULTIMATE TRUTH (don dam pa'i bden pa) The absolute nature of relative truth; that all phenomena are beyond arising, dwelling, and ceasing.

UNCONDITIONED BODY OF LIGHT (zag med 'od kyi lus) Same as rainbow body.

UNCONDITIONED COEMERGENT WISDOM (zag med lhan cig skyes pa'i ye shes) See coemergent wisdom.

UNEXCELLED ENLIGHTENMENT (bla na med pa'i byang chub) Complete and perfect buddhahood.

UNFAILING INTERDEPENDENCE OF CAUSE AND EFFECT (bslu med rgyu 'bras kyi rten 'brel) The law of relative truth.

UNIFIED LEVEL OF VAJRADHARA (zung 'jug rdo rje 'chang gi go 'phang) Synonymous with the state of complete enlightenment.

UNION DISSOLVING INTO WISDOM (zung 'jug ye shes la thim pa) One of the phases of the bardo of dharmata.

UNION OF SUN AND MOON TANTRA (nyi zla kha sbyor gyi rgyud) A Dzogchen tantra.

UNITY DISSOLVING INTO WISDOM (zung 'jug ye shes la thim pa) One of the phases of the bardo of dharmata.

UNPLEASANT SOUND (sgra mi snyan) The continent to the north of Mount Sumeru.

UPA (gnyis ka) The second of the three outer tantras.

VAIROCHANA (rnam par snang mdzad) (1) One of the five buddhas. (2) The great translator at the time of King Trisong Detsen (ninth century).

VAJRA FAMILY (rdo rje'i rigs)   One of the five families.

VAJRA MASTER (rdo rje slob dpon)   A tantric master who is adept in the rituals and meaning of vajrayana. The master from whom one receives tantric teachings.

VAJRA VEHICLE OF SECRET MANTRA (gsang sngags rdo rje'i theg pa)   *See* Secret mantra.

VAJRADHARA (rdo rje 'chang)   The dharmakaya buddha of the Sarma School.

VAJRASANA (rdo rje gdan)   The "diamond seat" under the Bodhi Tree in Bodh Gaya, where Buddha Shakyamuni attained enlightenment.

VASE EMPOWERMENT (bum pa'i dbang)   The first of the four empowerments.

VICTORIOUS ONE (rgyal ba)   Buddha Shakyamuni.

VICTORIOUS ONES (rgyal ba, jina)   Buddhas.

VICTORIOUS ONES AND THEIR SONS (rgyal ba sras bcas)   Buddhas and bodhisattvas.

VIDYADHARA (rig 'dzin)   "Knowledge-holder," holder [dhara] or bearer of knowledge [vidya]-mantra.

VIDYADHARA LEVEL OF SPONTANEOUS PRESENCE (lhun grub rig 'dzin gyi sa)   One of the stages during the bardo of dharmata.

VIMA   Short for Vimalamitra.

VIMALAMITRA (dri med bshes gnyen)   A Dzogchen master invited to Tibet by King Trisong Detsen.

WHEEL OF THE TWELVE LINKS OF INTERDEPENDENCE (rten 'brel yan lag bcu gnyis kyi 'khor lo).

WHITENESS (dkar lam)   An experience during the bardo of dying.

WHITENESS, REDNESS, AND BLACKNESS (dkar lam, dmar lam, nag lam)   The three experiences accompanying the stages of appearance, increase, and attainment.

WIND (rlung)   *See* prana.

WISDOM DAKINIS (ye shes kyi mkha' 'gro ma)   Enlightened female beings.

Glossary

WISDOM DISSOLVING INTO THE VIDYADHARA (LEVEL) OF SPONTANE-OUS PRESENCE (ye shes lhun grub rig 'dzin la thim pa)   One of the last experiences during the bardo of dharmata.

WISDOM OF EQUALITY (mnyam nyid ye shes)   One of the five wisdoms.

WISDOM WIND (ye shes kyi rlung).   The manifesting capacity of innate wisdom.

WISDOM-KNOWLEDGE EMPOWERMENT (shes rab ye shes kyi dbang)   The third of the four empowerments.

YAMA (gshin rje)   *See* Lord of Death.

YESHE TSOGYAL (ye shes mtsho rgyal)   The close female disciple of Guru Rinpoche and compiler of his teachings.

YIDAM (yi dam)   A personal deity and the root of accomplishment among the three roots.

YOGA (rnal 'byor)   The third of the three outer tantras: kriya, upa, and yoga.

YOGIN (rnal 'byor pa)   Male tantric practitioner.

YOGINI (rnal 'byor ma)   (1) Female practitioner. (2) Female manifestation appearing in the bardo of dharmata.

The Oral Instruction Given by the Great Vidyadhara of Immortality When His Physical Body Was About to Depart into Dharmadhatu.

AT ALL TIMES and in all situations, I bow to and take refuge in the sublime qualified master endowed with boundless compassion who is like a wish-fulfilling jewel! Please bestow your blessings upon me!

To attain the state of unexcelled enlightenment, upon entering the gate of the precious Buddhadharma, you must give up concerns for this life!

Your parents, family, friends and other people lead your mind towards the fleeting goals of this life's activities, involving you in countless temporary and ultimate schemes, and offering all kinds of seemingly affectionate advice. Fooling yourself with all this will only result in various hindrances for Dharma practice; so it is essential not to listen to their words!

Besides a qualified master you won't find anyone who can give genuine spiritual advice. If you want to truly practice the Dharma you must quickly make preparations for death. Besides that, someone who entertains many temporary and ultimate plans will not be able to be a Dharma practitioner. People nowadays may outwardly pretend to try and please everyone but that only proves they are possessed inwardly by Mara.

Place your trust in the Dharma and your master! Take mountain retreats and unpeopled valleys as your dwelling place! Give up clinging to the short-lived pleasures of food, clothes and the like! Cut your ties to close family members!

Cast away all hypocritical flattery and manipulation! Focus one-pointedly on whatever your master says! By doing so your Dharma practice will be pure.

In general, people nowadays fall under Mara's reign. In particular, fickle and indolent women don't follow the advice of their teachers and instead take guidance from their family. By doing so they postpone doing what they definitely should be doing now: studying and training in Dharma practice. They seem to be primarily caught up in pointless worldly activities, kowtowing to family and friends, and the like. Therefore take hold of the "rope to your nose" and don't listen to others!

Sincerely take to heart the fact that the time of death lies uncertain. Then, knowing that there is no time to waste, diligently apply yourself to spiritual practice!

Your parent's kindness can only be repaid through Dharma practice, there is no benefit in repaying them with mundane attainments. Your teacher's kindness can only be repaid by practicing meditation, nothing else will do.

You can only benefit sentient beings through the bodhi-chitta resolve and by making aspirations; comparatively any other immediate action is of little benefit. As for your vows and samayas, unless you take your own conscience as witness, you will only become a hypocrite even though you may maintain a superficially virtuous morality and exterior.

Remain in secluded valleys and mountain retreats, because any spiritual practice done among the masses will only get you caught up in one situation after another. If you fail to take control of your own mind, even though you may make many promises and take many vows, they will result in hardly any benefit at all.

Unless you realize the key point of natural awareness— that knowing one thing liberates all—you won't find any certainty in pursuing endless seemingly 'important' information.

To summarize all vital points: with the thought "I will surely die!" hasten your plans to practice the Dharma! Since a master is your only hope, supplicate him from your heart! Since all pleasure and pain, whatever befalls you, is a repayment from the past, don't entertain many plans! Treat good, evil and impartial people as being above you and always take the lowest seat!

Train in impartial pure perception and do not belittle others! Acknowledge your own faults and don't meditate on others' shortcomings! Since the vital point of all the teachings lies in your own mind, always scrutinize it's nature!

Cast away the fixation of rigidly meditating upon a reference point and instead release your awareness into carefree openness! Decide that whatever you experience is the playful expression of awareness; don't try to improve good or correct evil!

All experience is your own mind and this mind, free from arising and ceasing, is the identity of the trikaya guru. This guru is indivisible from your natural awareness. Its cognizant radiance encompasses all that appears and exists.

Since all of appearance and existence is the magical display of this single expanse of awareness, the "ultimate view" is to see your mind in utterly naked naturalness. "Meditation training" is to remain in this continuously. "Ensuing cognition" is when a thought is projected. "Post-meditation" ("ensuing attainment") is to recognize that projection. "Conduct" is to mingle walking, sitting, and all other activities with the state of awareness.

The indivisibility of meditation and post-meditation is to be continuously free from even a second of distraction or confusion, uninterrupted by gaps of stillness or thought occurrence. When perfected it is the indivisibility of appearance and mind, of self and others, of pleasure and pain, enmity and friendship, and of love and hate. In short, 'fruition' is to have perpetually exhausted all kinds of duality fixating concepts.

When that has happened, samsara and nirvana are purified into the space [of dharmadhatu] and you have realized the spontaneously present three kayas. This is called "attaining buddhahood," the "exhaustion of phenomena and concepts" or "becoming a siddha." This is the time of gaining mastery over birth and death and the physical elements, and when effortless compassion and activity spontaneously occur throughout the entire universe.

In brief, the basic cause of everything is nothing but your present natural awareness. Therefore the sublime key point is to continuously maintain your natural awareness throughout both day and night without any separation.

As for all the thoughts that do occur as the expression of this natural awareness, be they gross or subtle, don't analyze them and don't follow them either. Don't try to bring them back into your meditation or obstruct them. If you succeed in simply recognizing the sudden occurrence of a thought, then let be in just that.

When it happens that you do get involved in thoughts that recollect the past or entertain the future, then let be directly in awareness. If a thought pattern continues, there is no need for a separate antidote since whatever takes place is liberated by itself. What occurs spontaneously is the radiance of your own mind. To see it with vivid clarity is the essential instruction!

It is your mind's natural disposition to spontaneously reflect. Consequently, spend your life within this state of carefree and pervasive openness, of undistracted nonmeditation, of knowing one thing that liberates all—in which all that appears and exists is dharmakaya, samsara and nirvana are indivisible, and arising and liberation are simultaneous. If you spend your entire life in spiritual activities within this kind of state, in which the thinker and the object of thought are an undivided unity, there is not a single doubt that you will capture the 'stronghold of nonregression' in this very life.

> Wherever the person stays who has abandoned
>   all activities,
> That very place is the buddhafield.
> If you can supplicate without duplicity,
> All that appears and exists is then the guru's
>   mandala.

> As soon as you cut the root of the demon Ego-
>   clinging,
> You are permanently free from obstacles, misfor-
>   tune and Mara.
> The moment you understand that the guru is
>   indivisible from your own mind,
> The falsehood of seeming meeting and separa-
>   tion spontaneously collapses.

> Once you resolve that samsara and nirvana are
>   the display of awareness,
> Who is there to experience the pain of any lower
>   realm?
> When realizing that your natural awareness is
>   the primordially free dharmakaya,
> What is the point of entertaining hopes and
>   fears about the paths and bhumis?

> In the meeting of the already acquainted mother
>   and child luminosities,

What is the use of fearing the collapse of the
illusory body?
When dying, die within the primordially pure
space of luminosity!
While alive, there is nothing more important
than training in meditation with unflagging
constancy!

You may compare all the sutras, tantras and oral
instructions,
But the essence of realization is nothing other
than this!
The ultimate and essential heart advice is pre-
cisely this!
And my last words at death are also none other
than this!

All worthy ones who are devoted to me,
Don't pay lip-service to this, but assimilate its
meaning!
The experience of original wakefulness will then
dawn from within your hearts,
And you will arrive at buddhahood in a single
instant!

By whatever merit which might arise from this
advice
May all my old mothers, sentient beings filling
all of space, be liberated!
Mangalam.

༄༄ །འཆི་མེད་རིག་འཛིན་ཆེན་པོ་སྐུ་མི་མངོན་ཆོས་ཀྱི་
དབྱིངས་སུ་གཤེགས་ཁར་གནང་བའི་ཞལ་གདམས་བཞུགས་སོ།

‖

༄༄། །དཔལ་ཏུ་མེད་པ་སྲུགས་རྗེ་མཉམ་བའི་མཆོན་ལུན་བླ་དྲས་པ་ཡིད་
བཞིན་ནོར་བུ་ལྟ་བུ་ལ་དུས་དང་རྣམ་པ་ཐམས་ཅད་དུ་ཕྱག་འཆལ་ཞིང་སྐྱབས་སུ་
མཆིའོ། བྱིན་གྱིས་བརླབ་པར་མཛད་དུ་གསོལ། དེ་ཡང་བསྐུན་པ་རིན་པོ་ཆེའི་
སྐོར་ཞུགས་ནས་བླ་མེད་ཀྱི་བྱང་ཆུབ་ཐོབ་པར་བྱ་བ་ལ། ཆེ་འདི་བློས་བཏང་དགོས།
ཕ་མ་ཉེ་འབྲེལ་མཆེད་གྲོགས་སོགས་ཀྱི་གནས་སྐབས་ཆེ་འདིའི་བུ་བྱེད་ཀྱི་མདུན་
མས་བློ་བྱེད་ནས་འཕུལ་ཕུགས་ཀྱི་རྟིས་གདངས་མང་པོ་དང་ཁ་ཆ་ཡིན་ཡིན་འདུ་བའི་
གདུས་མང་པོས་མགོ་བསྐོར་ཏེ་ཆོས་ཀྱི་བར་ཆད་སྣ་ཆོགས་བྱེད་པ་འབྱུང་བས། དེ་
དག་གི་དགའ་ལ་མི་ཉན་པ་གལ་ཆེ། ཆོས་ཁ་དག་གི་ མདུན་མ་སྟོབ་མཁན་ནི་མཆན་
ལྟུན་གྱི་བླ་མ་མ་གཏོགས་མི་ཡོང་། ཆོས་ཡང་དག་ཞིག་བྱེད་ན་སྨྱུར་དུ་འཆི་གྲུབ་བྱེད་
པ་ཅིག་མ་གཏོགས་འཕུལ་ཕུགས་ཀྱི་རྟིས་དོག་མང་པོ་བྱེད་མཁན་ལ་ཆོས་ཡོང་བའི་
ཐབས་མེད། དེང་སང་གི་མི་རྣམས་དང་མཐུན་པར་བྱེད་མཁན་དེ་འཕུལ་དུ་ཡིན་
མདོགཁ་ཡང་། ཕུགས་ནས་བདུད་ཞུགས་ཆར་བའི་རྟགས་ཡིན། བློ་ཆོས་དང་བླ་

མ་ལ་བཀའ། སྟོད་ས་རི་ཁྲོད་ལྱུང་སྟོང་འགྱིམ། ཟས་གོས་སོགས་འཕྲལ་དུ་སྟྱིད་ཆོས་ཐམས་ཅད་ལ་ཞེན་པ་སྤུང་། ཏེ་འབྲེལ་གྱི་འཕྲི་བ་བཅད། དོ་བསྱུང་དང་མི་ཆོས་ཐམས་ཅད་རྒྱུན་ཏུ་སྤྱར། བླ་མས་ཅི་གསུངས་ལ་བློ་རྩེ་རིལ་བ་དེ་ཆོས་ཤ་དག ཡོང་བ་ཡིན། སྤྱིར་དེངས་སང་གི་མི་རྣམས་བདུད་དབང་ཏུ་གྱུར། དགོས་སུ་སྲྱི་བ དམན་པའི་བྱུད་མེད་རྣམས་ནི་སྲིང་རྱས་ཆུང་ཞིང་བསྱར་སྐྱ་བས་བླ་མའི་གདམས་པ་ལ་མི་ཉན་པར་ཏེ་འབྲེལ་གྱི་བློ་ཁྲིད་ལ་ཉན་ནས། དགོས་ངེས་ཤེས་པའི་ལྷ་ཆོས་དང་སྱོམ་བསྱུབ་ཏེ་ཕྱི་འཕོལ་ཏུ་བྱེ་ཏིད། དགོས་པ་མེད་པའི་འཇིག་རྟེན་གྱི་བྱ་བྱེད། གཉེན་འདུན་གྱི་དོ་བསྱུང་སོགས་བློ་ན་མང་པོའི་དབང་ཏུ་སོང་བ་ཁོ་ན་མང་བས་དེས ན་རང་གི་སྱ་ཐག་རང་གིས་བཟུང་ནས་གཞན་གྱི་ཁ་ལ་མི་ཉན། ནས་འཆི་ཆ་མེད སྱིད་ལ་བསམ་ལ། ཕོང་མེད་ཀྱི་བརྩོན་འགྲུས་དག་པོས་ཆོས་ལ་འབྱུངས། ཕ མའི་དྲིན་ལན་ཆོས་ཀྱི་མ་འཇལ་ན་འཇིག་རྟེན་གྱིས་འཇལ་བས་ཕན་པ་མེད། བླ་མའི སྐུ་དྲིན་དང་ཞབས་ཏོག་སྱོམ་བསྱབ་ཀྱིས་མ་འཇལ་ན། གཞན་གྱིས་སྱུ་དྲིན་མི་འཕོར། སེམས་ཅན་ལ་ཕན་པ་ཡང་སེམས་བསྱེད་སྱོན་ལས་ཀྱིས་མ་གཏོགས་དངོས་སུ་ཕན རྒྱུ་ཆུང་། སྱོས་པ་དས་ཆིག་རང་སེམས་དབང་ཏུ་བཙུག་པ་ཞིགས་བྱུང་ན། ཕྱར སྱང་གི་བཅུན་ཆོགས་དང་ཁྲེལ་དོ་ཆ་སོགས་ཀྱང་དོ་ལྷོག་ཅན་ཞིག་མིན་པ་མི་ཡོང་། ལྱང་སྱོང་རི་ཁྲོད་མ་འགྱིས་ན་མི་མང་ཁྲོད་ཀྱི་དགེ་སྱོར་དེ་ཉེན་དབང་ཏུ་ཕོར་བ་འས ཆེ། རང་སེམས་ཀྱི་ཁ་ལོ་རང་གིས་བསྱུར་མ་ཐུབ་ན། ཁས་ལན་དས་བཅན་མང ཡང་ཕན་པ་དགའན། རང་རིག་གཅིག་ཤེས་ཀུན་གྲོལ་གྱི་གནད་དོན་མ་ཏོགས་ན། ཤེས་ཤེས་དགོས་དགོས་ལ་ཕག་ཆོད་རྱུ་མི་ཡོང་། འབག་དོན་ཏྲིལ་གྱིས་ཏྲིལ་ན

སྱུར་དུ་འཆི་བར་ཐག་ཆོད་ནསམ་པས་བློ་རྣ་ཆོས་ལ་བསྱུང་། བླ་མ་མ་གཏོགས་རེ་
ས་མེད་པས་སྙིང་ནས་གསོལ་བ་གདབ། སྱིད་སྱུག་གང་བྱུང་སྱོན་གྱི་བསྱོར་ཆད་
ཡིན་པས་བློ་རྣ་མ་མང་། བཟང་ངན་འབྱིང་གསུམ་གོང་དུ་ཁྱར་ལ་དམན་ས་ཁོན་
བཟུང་། དག་སྱུང་སྱོགས་མེད་སྱུང་ཞིང་གཞན་ལ་སྱར་པ་མི་གདབ། རང་སྱོན་རང་
གིས་དོགས་པར་བུ་ཞིང་གཞན་སྱོན་མི་བསམ། ཆོས་ཀྱན་གཉད་འགག་རང་སེམས་
ལ་ཡོད་པས་སེམས་ཉིད་ལ་ལྱ་དོགས་རྒྱུན་དུ་བྱ། དགྱོགས་གཏད་འཛུར་བསྱོམ་གྱི་
འཛིན་པ་སྱངས་ཏེ། རིག་པ་གྱ་ཡངས་སུ་སྱོད། གང་འཕར་རིག་པའི་རོལ་རྩལ་དུ་
ཐག་བཅད་ལ་བཟང་ངན་གྱི་བཆོས་སྱད་མི་བྱ། ཅིར་སྱང་ནི་རང་སེམས་སྱི་འགགག
མེད་པ་དེ་ནི་སྱ་གསུམ་ལྱ་མའི་དོ་བོ། བླ་མ་ནི་རང་གི་རིག་པ་འདི་གདང་དབྱེར་
མེད། དེའི་གསལ་མདངས་ནི་སྱང་སྱིད་ཀྱན་ལ་ཁྱབ། སྱང་སྱིད་ཐམས་ཆད་ནི་
རིག་པའི་ཀྱོང་གཅིག་པུའི་རྣམ་འཕུལ་ཡིན་ཆེ་སེམས་རང་བབས་ཏེན་ཆེ་རེ། རིག་པ་
ནི་ལྱ་བའི་མཐར་ཐུག ཀྱེའི་དང་དུ་འགྱ་དོག་མེད་པར་གནས་པ་ནི་སྱོམ་པའི་མཆས་
བཞག འབྱོ་བ་ནི་ཇེས་ཉེས། འབྱོ་བ་དངས་ཇེན་པ་ནི་ཇེས་ཐོག འབྱོ་འདུག་དང་
བུ་བྱེད་ཐམས་ཆད་རིག་ཐོག་ཏུ་བསྱེ་བ་ནི་སྱོད་པ། གནས་འགྱའི་བར་མཆམས་མེད་
པར་རྒྱན་དུ་ཡེངས་འཕུལ་སྱད་ཆིག་ཀྱང་མེད་པར་གྱར་པ་ནི་མཆམ་ཇེས་དབྱེར་མེད།
དེ་ཉིད་མཐར་ཕྱིན་པས་སྱང་སེམས་དབྱེར་མེད། བདག་གཞན་དབྱེར་མེད། བདེ་
སྱག་དགྱ་གཉེན་ཆགས་སྱང་སོགས་མདོར་ན་གཉིས་འཛིན་གྱི་དོག་པ་མཐའ་དག
གཏན་ནད་དུ་སོད་བ་ནི་འབྲས་བུ་སྱེ། དེ་ལྱར་གྱར་ཆེ་འཁོར་འདས་དབྱིངས་སུ་དག
ནས་སྱ་གསུམ་སྱན་གྲུབ་མདོན་དུ་བྱས་པ་དེ་ལ། སངས་རྒྱས་ཐོབ་པའི་ཆོས་ཇད་བོ

ཟད་གུབ་པ་ཐོབ་པ་ཞེས་ཟེར་ཏེ། སྐྱེ་འཆི་དང་འབྱུང་བ་ལ་རང་དབང་ཐོབ་ཅིང་
ཐུགས་རྗེ་དང་ཕྲིན་ལས་ཚོལ་མེད་དུ་ནུས་མཁན་དང་མཉམ་པ་ཤུགས་ཀྱིས་འབྱུང་བ་
སྟེ། མདོར་ན་དེ་ཐབས་ཅད་ཀྱི་རྒྱུའི་དོ་བོ་ནི་དམྱལ་བ་རང་རིག་འདི་ཁོ་ན་ཡིན་པས།
འདི་ཉིད་དང་མི་འབྲལ་བ་ཞིག་ཉིན་མཚན་ཀུན་ཏུ་སྐྱོང་བ་ནི་གནད་དུས་པ་ཡིན།
དེའི་སྐྱལ་ལས་རྣམ་པར་དོག་པ་སྤུ་རག་ཅི་འར་ཐམས་ཅད་ལ་བརྟགས་དཔྱད་ཡང་མི་
བྱ། རྗེས་སུ་ཡང་མི་འབྲང་། སྤོམ་ཐོག་ཏུ་ཆུར་བསྲུ་བའམ། བཀུག་པ་ལྟ་བུ་ཡང་
མི་བྱ་བར་རྣམ་རྟོག་ལས་ཀྱིས་འཕར་བ་དེ་ཀ་དོ་ཉེས་ཚོལ་བྱུང་ན་དེ་ཁར་སྐྱུར། སྐྱུར་
འདས་རྗེས་འབྱུང་དང་མ་འོངས་པ་མ་དྲན་བསུ་ལྱུ་བུའི་བསམ་པ་རྣམ་འཕར་ཀུང་རིག་
ཐོག་ཏུ་གཅེར་གྱིས་བཞག །ཐོག་པ་འཕོ་མཐུད་ན་གང་འཕར་རང་གྲོལ་ཡིན་པས་
གཉེན་པོ་གཞན་མི་དགོས། ཐོལ་གྱི་འཕར་བ་རང་སེམས་ཀྱི་མདངས་ཡིན། ཉིག་གེ་
རིག་པ་གདངས་དག་གི་གནད་ཡིན། ཆམ་གྱི་འཕྲོ་བ་ཁོ་རང་གི་ངང་ཆོལ་ཡིན་པས
དེ་ལྟུ་བའི་གུ་ཡངས་ཁྱབ་གདལ། སྣང་སྲིད་ཆོས་སྐུ་འཁོར་འདས་གཉིས་མེད།
འཕར་གྲོལ་དུས་མཉམ། སྤོམ་མེད་ཡེངས་མེད། གཅིག་ཤེས་ཀུན་གྲོལ་འདི་ལྟུ་བུའི་
དང་ནས། སྤོ་བུ་སྤོ་བྱེད་བྱུང་འདྲག་གི་དགེ་སྦྱོར་ལ་མི་ཆ་རྡིལ་བར་བྱས་ན། ཆ
འདི་ཉིད་ལ་ཕྱིར་མི་ལྡོག་པའི་བཙན་ས་ཟིན་པར་གདོན་མི་ཟའོ། བྱ་བ་སྙིང་ནས
ཐོངས་པའི་གང་ཟག་ལ། གར་འདུག་སངས་རྒྱས་ཞིང་ཁམས་དེ་ཁ་རང་། ཁ་ཞེ
མེད་པར་གསོལ་བ་འདེབས་ནུས་ན། སྣང་སྲིད་ལ་ལུས་བླ་མའི་དཀྱིལ་འཁོར།
ལགས། བདག་འཛིན་འགོང་པོ་རྟུ་ནས་ཆད་ཚོ་ན། བར་ཆད་ཀྱི་དབང་བདུད
དང་གཏན་ཐུག་ཡོད། བླ་མ་རང་སེམས་དབྱེར་མེད་གོ་བའི་ཚེ། འདུ་འབྲལ་སྐྱོང

བའི་རྟེན་ཕྱགས་རང་སར་རྟོལ། འཁོར་འདས་རིག་པའི་རོལ་པར་ཐག་ཆོད་ན།
དན་སོང་སྤུག་བསྲུབ་གང་དུ་སུ་ཡིས་སྟྲོང་། རང་རིག་ཆོས་སྐུ་ཡེ་གྲོལ་རྟོགས་ནས
ནི། ས་ལམ་རྟོད་རྡགས་རེ་རྡོགས་ཅི་ལ་བྱ། ཕོད་གསལ་སྣང་འཛིས་མ་བུ་འཕྲོད
པ་ལ། སྣ་ལུས་ཞིག་པའི་འཆོར་བག་ཅི་ལ་བྱེད། ཕྱི་ཡང་ཀ་དག་འོད་གསལ
དབྱིངས་སུ་ཤི། གསོན་རིང་སྒོམ་སྒྲུབ་ཞང་སྟོད་མེད་པ་གཅེས། མཆོ་རྒྱུད་མན་
དག་ཐམས་ཅད་ཞལ་སྲུ་ཡང་། དགོངས་པའི་སྙིང་པོ་འདི་ལས་གཞན་མ་མཆིས།
རྡོན་གྱི་སྙིང་གཏམ་མཐར་ཐུག་འདི་ཀ་རང་། ཤི་བའི་ཁ་ཆེམས་ཟེར་ཡང་འདི་ལས
མེད། བདག་ལ་མོས་གུས་བྱེད་པའི་སྐལ་ལྡན་ཀྱུན། འདི་ལ་ཁ་བྱེར་མ་བྱེད་དོན་
ལ་ཕོབ། ཉམས་སྟོང་ཡེ་ཤེས་སྟིང་གི་ནང་ནས་འཆར། སངས་རྒྱས་ས་ལ་སྐྱོད་
ཅིག་བསྐྱེད་པར་འགྱུར། དེ་ལྲར་གདམས་པའི་དགེ་བ་གང་དེ་ཡིས། མ་ནན་
མཁའ་ཁྱབ་འགྲོ་བ་སྐྲོལ་བར་ཤོག །ཟང་གལོ། ༈